FOLLOWING JESUS

A Disciples Walk
Through The Book Of Mark.

By Hans Martens

"As I read through *Following Jesus,* I recognized the keen mind and of its author. It is a very readable, pastoral, and practical walk through the Book of Mark that will benefit those who are seeking to understand how to live out their faith and those who want solid material to share with those who are new to Christ. I have had the privilege of serving alongside Hans Martens as a prairie pastor, in denominational leadership, and doing pastoral training and development in Africa. In this book I see the same deep walk with God that I've seen every time I have ministered with the author. Every careful reader will find helpful instruction for living and making disciples brought to life out of the Book of Mark through Han's work. Well done my friend!"

-JOHN DRISNER, former Superintendent of the Saskatchewan PAOC district and currently Senior Pastor of Lawson Heights Neighbourhood Church.

"Hans Martens' book is a concise and captivating read on the truth of the Gospel of Jesus. Hans leads us on a simple path to following the narrative of Salvation and Freedom through Christ. This is a great book to read, reread, and pass on to anyone interested in a deeper understanding of a journey with Christ."

-CAROLYN NEARY, International and National award-winning. Coauthor *of A View From Heaven*

"Drawing on years of ministry experience, Pastor Hans Martens presents a personal and pastoral path to discipleship that is gentle, loving, and accessible to all."

-JEROMEY MARTINI, Ph.D. President of Horizon College & Seminary

"In this book Pastor Hans Martens provides a key component of what is necessary if we are going to fulfill Jesus' mandate to go and make disciplined followers of Him. Jesus indicated disciple-making would include "teaching them to obey everything I have commanded you". In a thorough, systematic manner Hans walks through so many of the critical understandings one must learn to know if they are to be true disciples of Jesus. How he addresses the subjects is clearly rooted in the life of someone who pours his life into real people, both before they know Jesus personally and as they continue to follow Him after. Discipleship is a relationally based process and this book captures that.

If we are going to have beneficial resources to make disciples, they need to come from someone who is not only a hearer of the Word but a doer also. Thanks Hans for putting into words your years of experience as you have lived out the disciple-making mandate of Jesus in a personal, practical, and transformative manner."

-DAVID WELLS, General Superintendent – The Pentecostal Assemblies of Canada

"When one is focused on the Word and the leading of the Holy Spirit, a transformation and life change will happen. Many of the testimonials included in this book speak loud and clear of the power of the word and the illumination the Holy Spirit gives. May this book bless many readers and may their lives be transformed by the power of God."

-PAUL SOETOPO, Missionary to Indonesia

Dedication

I dedicate this book to Okimaw Ohci Healing Lodge.

Ten years ago, we the Maple Creek Family Church began a relationship with the nearby First Nations women's prison. The residents there did community service every week by helping clean the church and helping make Tuesday night community suppers. Every Saturday two of us from the church were permitted to go to the prison to host a Bible study. I was blessed with having the opportunity to work with the residents and staff. I often dreamed of having something in my hand that I could bring to explain who Jesus is and what His disciples would look like today, and from that inspiration I wrote this book.

Acknowledgements

I want to thank my wife Janet, and daughter Janelle for reading through the manuscript making suggestions and corrections. I want to thank Connie Phillips for editing and preparing it for printing. I also want to thank all who endorsed the book.

Table of Contents

1. Follow Jesus!

Find a bible! Get one if you don't have one. Read the Gospel of Mark Chapter 1.

Jesus called us to make disciples of all nations.   A disciple is a student, and someone who is willing to follow someone else.   As we see in Mark 1, Jesus picked Andrew and Simon to follow Him; a little later, He invited John and James to come with Him, and eventually the rest of the twelve were chosen. Like universities of today, students had to apply to the rabbis and if accepted they could become students, but not with Jesus.   Unlike the contemporary teachers or rabbis, Jesus did not take applications -- He chose His own. He certainly used different criteria, and I am not sure which since the ones He picked seemed the unlikely candidates.   These chosen ones included uneducated ordinary fishermen, a despised tax collector and a zealot (that is, a terrorist).

My first question is why did they follow Him? James and John left their father's business just like that, apparently, no questions asked. What happened?

I suggest two answers. First, I believe that John the Baptist had prepared them. John the Baptist was a forerunner preparing the coming of the Messiah. This man who wore strange clothing and ate unusual food preached repentance, declaring that the Kingdom of God was near. People came from Jerusalem and from all over Judea to hear Him, and He baptized the ones who repented. According to the Gospel of John, John the Baptist had heard from God that the Messiah would be the One upon whom the Holy Spirit descended. (John 1:33) In the beginning of Mark, Jesus met John the Baptist and asked him to baptize Him. As Jesus came out of the water, the Holy Spirit came on Jesus, a clear sign that this was the Messiah. I believe there is a good chance that John the Baptist had already told the four disciples that Jesus was the coming Messiah.

Like the four disciples, you might also have had a 'John the Baptist' come and prepare the way for you to meet Jesus. Someone might have told you about Him, causing you to be curious and eager to know more. Maybe you are at that stage where you are not sure, but if you could, you would gladly go with a friend and meet Him. The most incredibly good news is that even though Jesus is not here in physical form, you can meet Him. Jesus is not a myth, He is not a concept, and He is not dead. Jesus is alive and has made a way for us to encounter Him as a person.   Yes, it is a mystery, but nonetheless real.   Stay with me and I will show you how to meet Him. My point is that it often takes someone else to lead you to that encounter; just as God used John the Baptist to lead the four disciples to Jesus, in the same way God might use another person to lead you to Him.

The second reason and the most important reason that they followed Him was because of what the Bible says in Mark 1:22: "Jesus taught with authority and not as the teachers of the law." As I understand, the Greek word used for authority comes from the word "author". Jesus did not quote other learned men as the teachers of the law did; rather, He spoke as if the words came from Him, emanating truth and love.

John Ortberg, in his book Faith and Doubt, tells a story of a famous psychologist, Dr. Lee Edward Travis. This man was considered among the thirteen most influential psychologists in mid-twentieth century. He had not been in a church for forty years. One day at 65 years of age, he stepped into a church for no other reason but to try it out. There, sitting in a pew, he had a full-blown experience with Jesus. It so transformed him that for the next 25 years, he led a doctoral program for Christians in Clinical Psychology. What happened? He encountered the truth through the Presence of the living God and His Word. This truth of an invisible God, who is as real as the chair you are sitting on, was not discovered through studying, but through encountering His Presence. Jesus' words carry an anointing or Presence with them that draws you to Him, and for that reason I believe the four disciples, as well as Dr. Travis, ended up following Him.

The other question coming from this text is what does that have to do with you and me? The truth is that Jesus is also calling you to follow Him. You may ask, "Why should I? Besides, how can I since He is invisible?" I am glad you asked.

My observation is that we all follow someone or something; the real question becomes who do you want to follow? When we are young, we follow our dreams and chase the rainbows, but as someone who has lived through half a century, I can truly say that many of those dreams don't live up to their promises. What we rarely recognize is that we often do not choose whom we want to follow; we simply flow with the culture in which we live and respond to the values imposed upon us.

Going with the flow starts early, as evidenced by watching the teenagers. Most teens eventually distance themselves from their parents and decide, "I am not going to listen to them anymore. I am my own master." But all they really do is follow another group. They simply shift from their parents' influence to their peers; just look at their clothes: 90% of teens seem to wear the same thing. I grew up as an atheist and I was convinced that I had found the truth. The way I saw it, there was only 'matter' and no Creator God. (Unlike many of my friends, I ended up reflecting a great deal about what I believed, maybe hoping that that way I would sound like a deep thinker. I truly considered the consequences for this belief system). We came from nothing and we went to nothing and everything in between was merely coincidence. My only purpose for living was to survive. Are you happy yet?

Looking back, however, I eventually realized that what I believed was merely what my culture declared. From my parents to my teachers, from the media to my schoolbooks, from friends to my heroes, the message was the same: "There is no God; therefore evolution is the only answer to where we came from." For that reason, I never questioned my belief system. Why should I?

The problem with this type of belief system is that you might follow someone or something, but in the end, you realize that the blind were leading the blind, which may, as Jesus declared, "lead you into the pit" (Luke 6:39), and not onto the mountains of success as you dreamed.

But what is this pit? It is living a life striving for something that offers significance, pleasure, purpose and hope, but it turns out to be a shadow. There is nothing wrong with pursuing a career or a sport or a business venture, but if that is all that you draw your identity and destiny from, then one day you will discover that you are mortal, and things are perishable. The pit, like an idol, is lifeless and provides no answers or satisfaction, but demands your worship. I was just reading a story about Daryl Strawberry, the famous baseball player from the mid 1980's to the end of 1990. Daryl signed an 8-million-dollar contract by the time he was 21 years of age, and he won four World Series games. But the pressure drew him to drugs and in the end; he lost it all so that he could gain everything. In his desperation he completely surrendered to Jesus. Today, Daryl and his wife are pastors and run a treatment center. The pit comes eventually to all of us if we do not follow the call and follow the One who holds our future in His hands. Jesus declares:"23 Then he said to them all: "Whoever wants to be my disciple must deny themselves and take up their cross daily and follow me." (Luke 9:23)

Why should you follow Jesus? Jesus makes the claim that: "6 ...I am the way and the truth and the life. No one comes to the Father except through me." (John 14:6). Follow Him for two good reasons: first, because Jesus is the truth and second, because He holds the answers to the four key questions that every human faces whether they consciously ask them or not. These questions are: Where do I come from? Why am I here? Who am I? And where am I going? Jesus defines the human dilemma, and He offers a

13

solution. As humans, we have all fallen short of His glory. Because of sin we are missing the mark, we are guilty, we are lost and in need of a Saviour. Jesus came into the world to live the life we should have lived; that is, a life that is completely dependent on God the Father. Jesus died the death that we should have died, because we deserved the wrath that Jesus took on the cross. Because of Jesus' death for our sins, we can be free from our past and receive a new life. This is a life that springs from a unique relationship to the triune God. Through Jesus' sacrifice, we receive the Holy Spirit, who empowers us to follow God as His sons and daughters. This ability to follow Him is not based on our good efforts, our qualifying works or our great efforts, but on His grace.

At the beginning of Jesus' ministry, we see Philip going to find Nathan. Nathan is found and Philip declares that he should come with him because he has found the man that Moses and the prophets spoke about. "Come and see Jesus from Nazareth." Nathan answered, "Can anything good come from Nazareth?" Philip answered, "Come and see." (John 1:46) You may not be ready to follow but why don't you come and see for yourself? God will reward anyone who earnestly seeks Him, as He did to the Washington Post investigative reporter, Lee Strobel. Lee set out to disprove his wife's belief in the Bible. After two years of research, he could not deny the overwhelming evidence that supports the truth of Jesus' crucifixion and resurrection and the reliability of the Bible. His testimony has been turned into a movie called "The Case for Christ".

So how can you follow? The four fishermen had to let go of their livelihood and trust Jesus to lead them. To follow Jesus, you must sense the call or invitation. This awareness of your need for Jesus might come from a sermon, a word from the Bible or a friend like Philip who invites you to investigate. You might pray a prayer of repentance and ask Jesus to be your Lord. That is great, but more is required. The Bible talks about being transformed. The Greek word is metamorphosis. Paul writes in 2 Cor. 3:18 that when we turn to Jesus we are being transformed into His image. This is like the process of a caterpillar being transformed into a butterfly. This process becomes easier the more we are willing to let go of the things of this world that we hang onto. If money is your god, the Holy Spirit will help you let go of your attachment to your security coming from money. If sports are more important than Jesus, you must place that diversion onto the altar. If alcohol is your idol, ask Jesus to help you be free. If you are living with your girlfriend, you might need to move out until you are married.

Danish Philosopher Soren Kirkegaard says that you need to make a leap of faith. When Kirkegaard talks about a leap of faith, he is talking about commitment. A leap of faith is not a blind leap, you might have all the facts; nonetheless, there are some things you cannot experience unless you are completely committed. It is like marriage, you can know a lot about your fiancée but when you get married, you are making a leap. What she will be like in 20 years, you do not know. You trust that it will be good. There is no guarantee what the future holds, but at the same time you can never really experience marriage without the commitment. When you have a baby, you might read all about it, but it is not until you have the baby that you are committed and truly can say, "I now know what it means to be a parent." Yet there is no guarantee what that child is going to be like in fifteen years.

John Ortberg gives an illustration in his book Faith and Doubt about trapeze acrobats. They swing in the air from two ropes joined with a piece of dowel called a trapeze. At one point the first acrobat let's go of his trapeze and for a few seconds is suspended in the air until the second acrobat, at just the right time, grabs him and carries him to safety. Faith is like that. You must let go of your agenda and worldview to grab hold of God the Father's hands. It may feel very scary during the 'letting-go' of your past beliefs until you can feel secure in the hands of God. This choice to let go of your reputation, your agenda and what the world offers, is a choice you are asked to make to be able to identify with Jesus. As you let go of your soul-ish life, wrong values and belief systems, you will find abundant life. Jesus says in Matthew 16:24, "For whoever desires to save his life will lose it, but whoever loses his life for My sake will find it."Faith is not a feeling; it is a choice. This requires a prayer of surrender and a willingness to search the Scriptures for what Jesus wants you to do. When you sense the prompting of the Holy Spirit, be quick to obey. This process is a daily routine for anyone who follows Jesus.

Why did the disciples want to follow Jesus? What four key life questions does Jesus give answers to? Unlike the first 12 disciples, you cannot see Jesus, so how can you follow Him?

If you want to follow Jesus, here is a prayer you can pray:

Dear Jesus, I cannot save myself, I need You. I bring all my sin to You at the cross, along with my guilt, my shame, and my wrong choices. I have hurt You, other people and myself. I thank You, Jesus that You have paid my debt and forgiven me. Thank You, Jesus, as You rose from the dead so I could also rise from my past and receive a new identity. Today I choose to make You my Lord and Saviour, and I commit myself to follow You.

2. Call to Greatness

Read the Gospel of Mark Chapter 2

I just want to make a disclaimer. When we talk about being great, it is not greatness in the eyes of the world, but greatness in the eyes of God, because it is in Jesus that you become the greatest you can be. Therefore, the call to be great is not about being a better hockey player or businessman than someone else, it is to fulfill what God has called you to. In other words, it is not about competition, it is about being what the Maker of all has designed you to be.

"16 As Jesus walked beside the Sea of Galilee, he saw Simon and his brother Andrew casting a net into the lake, for they were fishermen.17 "Come, follow me," Jesus said, "and I will send you out to fish for people." 18 At once they left their nets and followed him.19 When he had gone a little farther; he saw James son of Zebedee and his brother John in a boat, preparing their nets. 20 Without delay he called them, and they left their father Zebedee in the boat with the hired men and followed him."(Mark 1)

I believe that everyone has a desire for significance. Life is not all about surviving by going from paycheque to paycheque, drinking beer and hanging out with the gang; it is about leaving an imprint on this earth in some way. We want to be noticed for having accomplished something. My two-year-old grandson tries to stand on his head by sticking his one leg up in the air while placing his head on the floor, at the same time calling, "Grandpa, Grandpa, Grandpa, look what I can do!"

Earlier I mentioned the two reasons why I believe that the disciples followed Jesus: one was that John the Baptist had already told them that Jesus was the Messiah, and the second reason was that Jesus emanated the Presence of God and He spoke with authority. In addition, I believe they followed Jesus because He offered an adventure into the unknown with potential of being something more than a fisherman. He offered them an answer to their very deep longing to be part of something bigger than what the world of fishing could ever offer. The disciples, just like the rest of us, thought it was all about them. James and John asked Jesus: "Let one of us sit at your right and the other at your left in your glory." (Mark 10:37) In other words, James and John were asking Jesus to make them His right-hand men. They were not shy or humble. Jesus did not rebuke them, but it did lead to a lesson: 41 When the ten heard about this, they became indignant with James and John. 42 Jesus called them together and said, "You know that those who are regarded as rulers of the Gentiles lord it over them, and their high officials exercise authority over them. 43 Not so with you. Instead, whoever wants to become great among you must be your servant, 44 and whoever wants to be first must be slave of all."(Mark 10)

In my opinion this is what Jesus is saying: "Yes, you are going to be great, but to become great you have to serve and become a slave to fulfilling the greatest need of all of humanity." It is not about you, but it becomes about the great One in you: Jesus in you, the hope of glory. Jesus tells them and us that the way to be significant on this earth is to meet the needs of others.

Jesus is calling them to be fishers of men, or in other words, to be His witnesses to the world. He did not call everyone; He called 12 designated ones. But why did he call these men, and how did He do it? To understand this calling, I want to use the Old Testament story of Abraham. (Just to clarify, God changed the name Abram to Abraham, signifying that he will become father of many nations, which is what the name means.)

Terah, Abram's dad, was taking his family from Ur of the Chaldeans to the land of Canaan, but when he came to Haran he settled down. It was as if God had called him to Canaan, the Promised Land, but before he got there, he stopped in a place where there were a lot of occult practices and false gods. Many people start out following God but then stop because of comfort or the peer pressures of the culture around them. The culture was not embracing the God of Adam and Eve, and any faith in the true God had probably almost died out until God called Abram.

So, it was no surprise that God's first call was: 'Now the Lord had said unto Abram, Get thee out of thy country, and from thy kindred, and from thy father's house, unto a land that I will shew thee:' (Genesis 12:1-2 (KJV)

The call of God always involves leaving the lifestyle or the very environment that entraps you to your past. The disciples had to leave the nets and their livelihood. I work with prison inmates every week and their greatest fear is that when they are released, they will go back to their old community and not be able to withstand the temptations. As an atheist turned Christian, I had to leave my old teachings behind, and even some of my old friends. The call requires that you leave something of the old so you can embrace the new.

Abraham's call was a radical one: "Go... to the land I will show you."(Acts 7:3) I can just imagine Abram going to Sarah: "Sarah, pack everything and gather up the servants and animals, we are going." She might have looked with a question mark, "Where?" Abram may have answered, "I don't know. We will make the map as we go. Get ready, we are going camping."

God's answer to Abram's question would probably be the same: "Where are we going, God?" God's answer, "Just trust me!" Later, when God promised Abram a child and Abram asked, "How? I am old, like 99 years!" God's answer would be the same, "Just trust me!" When Abram had a young teenage son and God asked him to sacrifice Isaac, Abram would have asked, "Why?" God would have answered, "Just trust me!" The reason that this is a radical call is that it is a call to trust in an invisible God. The call to the disciples to follow Jesus was no less radical. They had to learn to trust Jesus. Jesus' call to you is a radical call to learn to trust an invisible God by following His Word. Are you ready?

As with the disciples, Abram was not called because he was qualified; rather, it is the call that qualifies you. Abram was not perfect, and he did not need to be, but he needed to hear the call, and so do you. Jesus calls the imperfect, like you and me. Why would He call the disciples who were uneducated fishermen, a tax collector, a zealot, and others? He called them because He saw something in them and then He called it forth. God the Father called forth what He saw in Abraham. God's Son, Jesus, called forth what He saw in the disciples.

My own father called forth what he knew was in me. He wanted me to have courage so at 6 years of age he put me on a pony that suddenly decided to run away, and when it made a turn into the yard, I landed in the hedge headfirst. Before I decided never to get back on a horse, my father put me on the horse again. He wanted me to face my fears. Later at 12 years of age, my dad owned a camp for kids, where he hired 60-70 horses from different farmers for one dollar a day. When the horses came off the truck, it was my job to ride them and test how safe they were. Many times, I hit the dirt. My dad taught me how to drive two horses and then four. Even though I messed up many times, the message was always the same, "You can do it!" Another time when I was about 12 years of age my dad decided to teach me how to drive. I sat behind the steering wheel, with my dad beside me in my grandfather's old car and proceeded to drive the car out of the quonset and in between two brick buildings. The gas pedal went down too far, and my steering was less than perfect, so I hit the corner of the building, smashing the headlight. But one lesson I learned from the accident was that my dad didn't yell or blame me. He went to my grandfather and told him it was his fault, and he would pay for it. I learned that it was safe to fail, and I learned to face my fears and overcome them. My dad brought out the courage in me. This was the courage I needed to cross the Atlantic at age 19 with only $100 in my pocket and a Danish /English dictionary, as I barely spoke English.

The greatest message my dad left me, however, was not that I could do it, but rather the message of the call, "Find something you are willing to die for." Jesus said 34 ... "Whoever wants to be my disciple must deny themselves and take up their cross and follow me. 35 For whoever wants to save their life[a] will lose it, but whoever loses their life for me and for the gospel will save it. 36 What good is it for someone to gain the whole world, yet forfeit their soul?' (Mark 8)

When Jesus called the disciples, there was nothing in them that the world would have considered worthy to be great. The society would have seen them as poor, uneducated, and among some of them, society's most despised and hated--hardly among the upper elite. Still, Jesus saw what most could not see. When Jesus saw Peter, He saw a man with a rock-solid faith long before he ever displayed those characteristics. When Jesus saw the disciples, He saw them as the salt and light of the world. He saw them changing the world -- not a bad destiny for some low-life Jews.

When God saw Abram (that was Abraham's birth name), He saw him as great. "I will make you into a great nation, and I will bless you; I will make your name great..." (Gen 12:2) God was going to make Abram known as the father of faith. God could see what he was to become. This is what Apostle Paul declares about him in Romans 4:21. "Being fully persuaded that God had power to do what he had promised. 22 This is why "it was credited to him as righteousness." If you read Abram's story, you will see that Abram was not perfect; in fact, he was a coward and God had to correct him at two different occasions, twice he lied about his wife. In fear of losing his life, he told the king of Egypt that Sarah was his sister.

23

However, Abraham learned to trust God, a trust that was tested when God told him to kill his son.

Having a great name is not merely about what you do, but more importantly, it's about who you are behind closed doors. A great name is first and foremost built on character. Abraham lied, he disobeyed, and he created an Ishmael. Abraham in fear gave away Sarah. Just like Abraham, when we set out to follow Jesus, we have character flaws that God will correct and forget. Abram became known as the Father of Faith because he learned to trust God, and because he passed on a legacy.

Jesus had a mission or a purpose. His sermon, as described in Mark, was to "Repent and believe the good news!" In Luke 19:10 Jesus said, "For the Son of Man came to seek and to save the lost."Repenting means turning from anything that Jesus hates, and turning to everything Jesus loves. Being lost means we have no clear purpose or sense of identity; whereas being found is becoming what we were created to be: a child of God. Entering His Kingdom is really allowing Him to be our Lord, our boss. The good news is that we do not enter by our own efforts; we enter because of God's grace extended to us through the cross. I am a sinner who was forgiven; therefore, I cannot brag, I can only be thankful. On the other hand, I have confidence, because Jesus found me and bestowed His love on me so that I could become a child of God.

Saving the lost is the mission that He called the disciples to be part of when He said, "Come, follow Me, and I will send you out to fish for people." (Mark 1:17) It was this mission that God called Abraham to partake in when He said, "I will surely bless you...and through your offspring all nations on earth will be blessed, because you have obeyed me." (Genesis 22:17, 18) God had a plan to create a nation and through that nation He would reveal Himself to the world. It was through the descendants of Abraham that Jesus came. God made a covenant with Abraham, and Jesus made a new covenant with those who follow Him. To follow Jesus is more than to be saved or rescued; it is to embrace a mission that is of eternal significance. You are called to be a blessing by helping spread the Gospel to the ends of the earth. When you tithe, you help to spread the Gospel. When you are on a worship team, you help people to experience the Kingdom of God. When you give offerings to missionaries, you are joining Jesus in fulfilling the Great Commission. When you are volunteering at church, you are His hands and feet. When you invite a neighbour to church, you help bring the Good News to the earth. Being called to follow Jesus is being called to something great, magnificent, and eternal.

 What does it mean to be great in the Kingdom of God?

Jesus did not call you merely to be saved, but to fulfill a mission. What is Jesus' mission for you?

One day you are going to stand before Jesus. What might He ask you?

Pray: Dear Jesus, show me how I am significant in your Kingdom. Sometimes I feel unimportant and without value in my eyes and in the eyes of people. Show me, Lord, the significance I have in Your Kingdom. Am I a light? Show me how I can be more of a light.

3. The Authority of Jesus

Read the Gospel of Mark Chapter 3

Authority: the power to give orders or make decisions: the power or right to direct or control something. (Merriam Webster)

Let me recapture what happens at the beginning of the Gospel of Mark. John the Baptist introduces Jesus as the one who is going to baptize people with the Holy Spirit. Jesus shows up on the scene in the book of Mark when He is being baptized in the water and the Holy Spirit comes on Him. The Holy Spirit leads Jesus into the wilderness where Satan tempts Him. Unlike Adam, Jesus does not fall for the temptations (Luke 4:13). Jesus begins teaching, and the listeners are impressed because He teaches with authority. Then He calls the four disciples to follow Him. Remember that the disciples are experiencing Jesus before the cross. They know Jesus as the coming Messiah who will usher in a kingdom. They really do not know what that will look like or who the person of Jesus really is. By following Jesus' example, we can see how He made disciples and how we can do the same. Making disciples simply means helping people on their journey of faith and showing them how to apply the Word of God to their lives.

Jesus then sets out to display His authority to the disciples and the world. Authority is related to power, but it is not the same thing. A policeman has power in his pistol and his fist, but he has authority in his badge. If you ever come against an officer and disrespect his badge, the policeman has the law and the entire police force behind him, not just his fist and pistol. Jesus has power through the Holy Spirit, and He has authority as the Son of God. The authority of a policeman is directly related to the mission that he has; similarly, Jesus' authority is related to His Father's mission on earth as fulfilled through Jesus.

Mark 1:21 They went to Capernaum, and when the Sabbath came, Jesus went into the synagogue and began to teach. 22 The people were amazed at his teaching, because he taught them as one who had authority, not as the teachers of the law. 23 Just then a man in their synagogue who was possessed by an impure spirit cried out, 24 "What do you want with us, Jesus of Nazareth? Have you come to destroy us? I know who you are—the Holy One of God!"

25 "Be quiet!" said Jesus sternly. "Come out of him!" 26 The impure spirit shook the man violently and came out of him with a shriek.

27 The people were all so amazed that they asked each other, "What is this? A new teaching—and with authority! He even gives orders to impure spirits and they obey him." 28 News about him spread quickly over the whole region of Galilee."(Mark 1:21-27)

Now imagine being one of the disciples. You have left behind your livelihood, at least for the time being, and this is what you hear and see.   The first thing you see is Jesus, teaching in a synagogue in Capernaum. (Pieces of that synagogue are still there today.)   While he is teaching, you hear a demon-possessed man shouting, "24 What do you want with us, Jesus of Nazareth? Have you come to destroy us? I know who you are—the Holy One of God!"(Mark 1:24)

The first one to declare who Jesus is was a demon.   Yes, you heard that right. I believe this is further evidence of the historical accuracy of the Bible. If this were fiction, the author would never have chosen a demon to declare the truth. He would have chosen someone important with influence and status, not a demon. The disciples are spectators, and you can imagine their eyes as big as saucers, mine would have been too! They are spellbound, and they might be thinking, "Who is he?" In our culture people rarely ask about what is the truth; they ask for help. Instead, they wonder if Jesus can help them with their issues.   Many do come to Jesus through a crisis, but if all you have is an experience and not the truth, then your faith will not stand the storms.   You need to know who Jesus is. He is either God or He is not.

What about you? Do you know Him as God? Jesus is about to show the disciples and all of us who read the Gospel of Mark, who He is. Where did the demons learn about Jesus? They knew Him because of where they came from. Satan was a fallen angel who had lived in heaven and because of his rebellion, God threw him out. This is what is written in Isaiah 14:12 "How you have fallen from heaven, morning star, son of the dawn!" Satan was a created being who had lived in the same Kingdom where Jesus lived.   Some believe that just as Satan was a fallen angel, so were the demons. Whether that is true or not, we know this: the demons are under the authority of Satan. They come from a spiritual realm that Jesus is about to reveal. Jesus tells the demon to be quiet and then tells the spirit to leave. The man convulses and the unclean spirit leaves. Jesus demonstrates His authority over the demon as he sets a man free by a mere command. They are wondering, "What is this? A new teaching—and with authority! He even gives orders to impure spirits and they obey him." (Mark 1:27)

The next step of authority is Jesus' power over sickness. Because of this display of deliverance, a huge gathering follows Jesus to Simon and Andrew's house, where Simon's mother-in-law lies sick with fever. Jesus' authority over sickness is displayed: as He touches her, the fever leaves. The news goes out quickly and many sick and demon-possessed people are brought to Him. Nothing like this has been seen in all of Judea. Jesus is our healer.

One scene follows another as Jesus takes authority over a common illness of leprosy. A leper comes to Jesus asking for help:

40 A man with leprosy came to him and begged him on his knees, "If you are willing, you can make me clean." 41 Jesus was indignant. He reached out his hand and touched the man. "I am willing," he said. "Be clean!" 42 Immediately the leprosy left him, and he was cleansed. (Mark 1)

This leper had faith. He knew that Jesus could heal if He was willing. At the time Jesus walked the earth, a leper was never to be near the general population, and they were never to touch another person. They were isolated from their community by being placed in compounds outside cities. If they wandered away from their designated area, they were to ring a bell or cry out, 'leper'. Therefore, when Jesus not only healed the leper but also touched him, Jesus displayed His authority, compassion and willingness to heal. Once again, Jesus goes back to Capernaum to teach and heal. This is His third example of authority over illness, but this time Jesus also illustrates His authority to forgive sin.   This is what happened:

Mark 2 A few days later, when Jesus again entered Capernaum, the people heard that he had come home. 2 They gathered in such large numbers that there was no room left, not even outside the door, and he preached the word to them. 3 Some men came, bringing to him a paralyzed man, carried by four of them. 4 since they could not get him to Jesus because of the crowd, they made an opening in the roof above Jesus by digging through it and then lowered the mat the man was lying on. 5 When Jesus saw their faith, he said to the paralyzed man, "Son, your sins are forgiven."

6 Now some teachers of the law were sitting there, thinking to themselves, 7 "Why does this fellow talk like that? He's blaspheming! Who can forgive sins but God alone?" 8 Immediately Jesus knew in his spirit that this was what they were thinking in their hearts, and he said to them, "Why are you thinking these things? 9 Which is easier: to say to this paralyzed man, 'Your sins are forgiven,' or to say, 'Get up, take your mat and walk'? 10 But I want you to know that the Son of Man has authority on earth to forgive sins." So, he said to the man, 11 "I tell you, get up, take your mat and go home." 12 He got up, took his mat and walked out in full view of them all. This amazed everyone and they praised God, saying, "We have never seen anything like this!" (Mark 2)

Jesus was preaching and the room was packed. I have been in a mud hut in Kenya, Africa, where the diameter was merely 20 feet and it felt like a hundred people were crowded like sardines in there. As Jesus was teaching, the roof began to open. Four people desperately tried to get their friend before Jesus. Those four friends had faith. They must have seen Jesus do miracles before. (Would you like to have friends like those four? Friends who are willing to be embarrassed and humiliated in public by digging through a roof and lowering you down in front of a crowd.) Are you willing to risk taking a friend to church, to witness to them or bless them with a prayer? How far are you willing to go?

The crippled man is lowered through the roof and the crowd is anticipating a miracle. Jesus can do it, they have seen it before. Anticipation is great and the four friends are convinced that their friend lying on the mat will walk out. Then Jesus shocks everyone with these words, "Your sins are forgiven." What happened to the miracle? What happens when you are expecting one thing but get something different? Jesus knows that what we ask for and what we need might be two different things. Once I asked for Jesus to grow our church, and then I find myself at a women's prison doing Bible studies, and every Sunday hauling inmates to church. God answered, but not in the way expected. A healing is temporary, but a forgiven soul is eternally saved.

Jesus takes authority over guilt, to the surprise of the religious crowd. What is the problem here? This is what the teachers of the law were thinking in Mark 2: 7 "Why does this fellow talk like that? He's blaspheming! Who can forgive sins but God alone?" They were right, only God can forgive. Let us say I punch Peter and Andrew steps up and says, "I forgive you". My initial reaction would be, "What did I do to you, Andrew?" The point being made is that when we hurt someone or talk bad about someone, then we are hurting Jesus. God grieves when in our hearts we talk bad about someone. In the same way God is angry when we trust other things or people more than Him for our needs to be met. Jesus then says 9 Which is easier: to say to this paralyzed man, 'Your sins are forgiven,' or to say, 'Get up, take your mat and walk'? 10 But I want you to know that the Son of Man has authority on earth to forgive sins." So, he said to the man, 11 "I tell you, get up, take your mat and go home." (Mark 2:9-10)

For Jesus, it seems easy either way, but for man it is impossible to forgive sins that have been committed against someone else. Only God can do that, and so Jesus demonstrates His authority to forgive by a physical miracle of healing.

What has just taken place? Jesus has revealed His authority through His teaching; it was authentic, anointed and captivating. He revealed His authority over the demonic by driving out unclean spirits, by healing and by forgiving sin. The authority to forgive sin is a way of demonstrating that Jesus is divine.

What Jesus is leading up to is to not only display His authority but to delegate that authority. In Genesis 1:28 God spoke to Adam and Eve and commanded them to multiply and take dominion. Unfortunately for all of us, Adam and Eve listened to Satan and his sly sales pitch, "you will be like God."(Gen 3:5) By believing Satan and disobeying God, they were no longer under the authority of God. It is like a teenager who no longer wants to listen to his parents. He thinks he knows better. You cannot have two bosses in a house, so since it is the parents' house, he must go. Adam and Eve had to go but when they went, they gave their authority over to Satan who wants to take dominion over the earth. In fact, Satan thinks he has the dominion of the earth, which is why he can tempt Jesus with offering Him all the kingdoms of the world. He said to

Him, "I will give you all their authority and splendour; it has been given to me, and I will give it to anyone I want to." (Luke 4:6) Where did Satan get that authority? Adam and Eve gave it to him by coming into agreement with him.

When Jesus came into this earth, He was described as the second Adam, a man who was fully human and was also going to be tested like the first humans. This time however, when Satan tempted Jesus for forty days, Jesus did not come into agreement with him as the first Adam did; instead, He countered Satan with the Word and the Spirit of the Word.

The disciples observed how Jesus' authority and power overcame the works of the enemy. Apostle Paul explains what Jesus did in Acts 10:38 "... how God anointed Jesus of Nazareth with the Holy Spirit and with power, and how He went about doing good and healing all who were under the tyranny of the Devil..." Jesus demonstrated who He was through healing, deliverance, teaching the truth and through the rebirth of sinners. In each case He was rescuing people from the dominion of darkness and bringing them into the kingdom of light. Col 1:13 explains, "He has rescued us from the dominion of darkness and brought us into the kingdom of light."

The disciples are learning and watching, but like in kindergarten, there comes a time for show and tell. It is your turn to show; however, the teacher will not just let you show, you must explain as well. "14 He appointed twelve[a] that they might be with him and that he might send them out to preach 15 and to have authority to drive out demons."(Mark 3.15)

Jesus sends them out to practice. These are His instructions: 5 He said to them "Go into all the world and preach the gospel to all creation. 16 Whoever believes and is baptized will be saved, but whoever does not believe will be condemned." (Mark 16) "7 As you go, proclaim this message: 'The kingdom of heaven has come near.' 8 Heal the sick, raise the dead, cleanse those who have leprosy, and drive out demons. Freely you have received; freely give."(Matthew 10:7-8) The point of this journey of revealing His authority to us is that one day we will do what He did.   The disciples were watching, but the time was coming when they were no longer merely observers. They could no longer remain in the stands cheering Jesus; they had to get into the game.

Even though Jesus was God, He was under the authority of His Father. Jesus declared that He could only do what He saw His Father doing. As a teenager, His parents found Him in the Temple and when they asked Him where He had been, He explained to them that He had to be about His Father's business. Having spiritual authority requires being under the authority of Jesus. Being a disciple means ministering out of Jesus' authority. In Acts Chapter 4 the disciples declared that it was in the name of Jesus that the crippled man was healed. It was under the authority of Jesus that the power was released through them.

Whose authority are you under? We are all under something or some one's influence. It is whoever you look up to that you will influence you. If you are an atheist, you will look to people who are of similar persuasion. If it is not a person that an atheist looks to for guidance, it is the teaching of humanism. People who do evil things such as shooting up a school often look to extremely hateful ideology, such as Nazism. As Christians, we give authority to the Bible and the Holy Spirit to influence us. Because we are Christians, we look to Jesus for our authority. The power to control and direct certain things depends who we give authority to. As a student, much of my ability to make decisions was limited to what my teachers taught me. Some give authority to the government; therefore, they see all their power limited to what their government gives them. The result is they hold the government responsible for all their problems. Jesus teaches the disciples that they will be able to do even greater things than what He did, simply by believing in Him, which is another way of saying that if they will give all authority to Him, they will do great works.

"12 Very truly I tell you, whoever believes in me will do the works I have been doing, and they will do even greater things than these, because I am going to the Father. 13 And I will do whatever you ask in my name, so that the Father may be glorified in the Son. 14 You may ask me for anything in my name, and I will do it."(John 14)

Who do you blame for your problems? Who do you look to for direction? Who have you given power to?

Whose authority is Jesus under? How did Jesus demonstrate His authority?

What authority does He want to give to you?

Pray: Dear Jesus, I want to obey you and you alone. Help me to know Your Word and apply it. Also, Lord may I know how to use the authority You have given me to destroy the work of the enemy.

.

4. Sabbath Rest

Read the Gospel of Mark Chapter 2

Join me on this journey of walking with the disciples, discovering who Jesus is. Jesus teaches with authority, He takes authority over sickness. He takes authority over demons and He forgives. He forgives as if all sin was sin against Him; thereby He is claiming to be God. He speaks and prays without saying, "thus says the Lord." Unlike prophets or teachers who would refer to the authority of God, Jesus seems to be that authority. Demons flee and people are healed with a mere command. This next journey is an encounter with opposition, but also an encounter with the truth of the Gospel of peace...

Mark 2:23 One Sabbath Jesus was going through the grain fields, and as his disciples walked along, they began to pick some heads of grain. 24 The Pharisees said to him, "Look, why are they doing what is unlawful on the Sabbath?"

25 He answered, "Have you never read what David did when he and his companions were hungry and in need? 26 In the days of Abiathar the high priest, he entered the house of God and ate the

consecrated bread, which is lawful only for priests to eat. And he also gave some to his companions." 27 Then he said to them, "The Sabbath was made for man, not man for the Sabbath. 28 So the Son of Man is Lord even of the Sabbath."

Again, Jesus is using this dialogue to reveal Himself. When Jesus declares that He is the Son of Man, who is the Lord of the Sabbath, He shocks the religious establishment; however, to the disciples and to us who read it, it is a revelation of truth. For us Gentiles, the name 'Son of Man' might just mean that He is human, but for a Jew, especially a Pharisee, it might mean something very specific. Jesus eventually does make it clear. When he is being interrogated by the High Priest, he asked Him if He was the Messiah, and after a pause Jesus gave them all they wanted when He answered: 62 "I am." ... "And you will see the Son of Man sitting at the right hand of the Mighty One and coming on the clouds of heaven."(Mark 14:62)

His identity as Son of Man is revealed in Daniel 7:3 "In my vision at night I looked, and there before me was one like a son of man, coming with the clouds of heaven. He approached the Ancient of Days and was led into his presence. 14 He was given authority, glory and sovereign power; all nations and peoples of every language worshiped him. His dominion is an everlasting dominion that will not pass away, and his kingdom is one that will never be destroyed."

I was just reading a book, No God but One, by an ex-Muslim, Nabeel Qureshi. Nabeel was an Islamic evangelist whose parents had emigrated from Iran to USA.   While studying medicine, a fellow student and friend whom he had tried to convert challenged him to research Jesus' claim to be God in the Gospels. Nabeel read through Mark and discovered the meaning of 'Son of Man' and came to see how the prophecy in Daniel could only be about Jesus, riding on the clouds in the way only God can. The Son of Man will be worshiped by all nations and language groups, yet only God can be worshiped (Exodus 34:14 "Do not worship any other god, for the Lord, whose name is Jealous, is a jealous God...") This Son of Man will usher in an eternal kingdom, and only God can do that. Jesus reveals Himself as God; however, that is understood only when we see Jesus as part of the Trinity. Nabeel gives the example of the difference between the president and himself. The president is much more important than Nabeel, but they are both humans. They are the same. The drawback with that analogy is that the president and Nabeel occupy different roles that are separate from each other, but that is unthinkable when it comes to the Godhead.

What I am saying is that by using the name the 'Son of Man', Jesus refers to Himself indirectly as God. Read Daniel 7:3 again; the Son of Man can only describe God because only God will be worshiped. There are places where Jesus refers to Himself as 'I am', which is the name God gives Himself when Moses asks who I shall say you are? God said to Moses, "I am who I am" (Exodus 3:14). Jesus refers to Himself as I am: I am the light of the world, I am the bread of life, I am the way, the truth and the life. I am the resurrection and the life. I am the Alpha and Omega. Before Abraham was, I am. Jesus didn't stop with the name 'Son of Man', He also says, "I am the Lord of the Sabbath" and thereby He is saying (as part of the Trinity), I am the One who wrote the Ten Commandments. Jesus is not just Lord over the Sabbath; He is the Lord of the Sabbath. Jesus knows more than anyone what the

Sabbath is all about because He, together with the Father and the Holy Spirit, designed it for the benefit of mankind.

I asked my wife what she thought that the Jews might believe about the Sabbath. This is what she said that it was by keeping the Sabbath that they were identified as Jews (see Ezekiel 20:19, 20). How did the world know they were Jews? They would know it by the people who kept the Sabbath. If they broke the Sabbath, they could not really be Jews. When Jesus set Himself up as the Lord of the Sabbath and then broke the Sabbath rules, they saw Him as a threat to their identity. In their minds the Messiah would have to keep the rules. What a shock to them when Jesus declared, "I am the Lord of the Sabbath". Jesus is thereby saying that He made those laws and it was they who missed the spirit behind the laws.-

Religious people opposed Jesus because He did not comply with their man-made laws. The Pharisees had made up 39 laws of what one must not do on a Sabbath, and picking grain was one of them. Jesus was not denying the Ten Commandments or negating the need for rest as prescribed in the law of the Sabbath; rather, He is saying that it was for the benefit of man's need for renewal, rest and re-focus. I remember my Old Testament professor telling a story about his trip to Israel. They were travelling in a bus down a back road on a Saturday when an orthodox Jew stopped them. It turned out that a breaker had switched off in the nearby kibbutz. Since it was the Sabbath, he was not allowed to flick it on, so he thought that if he could stop a bus full of Gentiles, he could get one of them to do it. This sounds ridiculous, and that is the point of Jesus' remark: "Sabbath was made for man, not man for Sabbath."

Let us walk with Jesus as He preaches in the synagogue and watch the reaction He gets.

Mark 3:1"Another time Jesus went into the synagogue and a man with a shrivelled hand was there. 2 Some of them were looking for a reason to accuse Jesus, so they watched him closely to see if he would heal him on the Sabbath. 3 Jesus said to the man with the shrivelled hand "Stand up in front of everyone."

4 Then Jesus asked them, "Which is lawful on the Sabbath: to do good or to do evil, to save life or to kill?" But they remained silent. 5 He looked around at them in anger and, deeply distressed at their stubborn hearts, said to the man, "Stretch out your hand." He stretched it out, and his hand was completely restored. 6 Then the Pharisees went out and began to plot with the Herodians how they might kill Jesus."

Again, Jesus upset them by breaking their rules. What was His crime? He healed a man's hand on a Sabbath. Jesus, as the maker of the law, summarized all commandments into two. He can do that because He is God. He is saying that we are to love God with all that we have and then love our neighbour as we love ourselves. You are to be as excited about the success of others as you are of your own. You are to be as concerned about your neighbours' failure as you are about your own. Therefore, Jesus sees the Sabbath as a help for us busy, preoccupied, distracted humans to take time to love Him in our worship and to do good to others and to ourselves by resting.

Spiritual Rest! Jesus, together with the Father and the Holy Spirit, institutes the Sabbath to give us physical rest. But Jesus takes it further and teaches us about a spiritual Sabbath rest. A rest that comes from receiving His grace and mercy. Mark 10:28 "Come to me, all you who are weary and burdened, and I will give you rest. 29 Take my yoke upon you and learn from me, for I am gentle and humble in heart, and you will find rest for your souls."

The religious people hate Jesus because He came to destroy religion.

I was doing pre-marriage counselling the other day. The groom was not a believer and had been hurt by the bride's parents. Her parents had been pastors and wanted desperately for the groom to be saved. Therefore, they inadvertently made him feel less worthy. I explained to him the difference between religion and the Gospel. Religion is like a ladder; you feel you need to climb up the ladder to reach God. Every step is an effort of religious activity that you hope will satisfy God. As you climb up, you look down upon the ones below you and you feel somewhat superior to those who have not achieved the same level of morality or spirituality as you. You have only a temporary feeling of peace when you see how far you have come in comparison to the ones below, but you are never at rest because you never sure how far you have to go to be accepted and pleasing to God.

The good news of the Gospel, on the other hand, is that Jesus came down the ladder and found you. He offered you forgiveness and a new life, not because of what you have done but because of what He has done. Jesus came down as the Lord of the Sabbath to invite you into an eternal rest. This rest that is offered from the Lord of the Sabbath is rest that comes from ceasing to strive. You know who you were, a sinner forever condemned, and you know who you are now, redeemed, forever forgiven, accepted as a citizen of Heaven, a child of God chosen and adopted by His blood. Your name is written in the Lamb's Book of Life.

The movie called 'Chariots of Fire' illustrates what spiritual rest looks like. Eric Liddel is born into a Scottish missionary family residing in China. He spends his university years in Scotland. Eric, a committed Christian, is a fast runner and he is scheduled to represent England in the 1924 Olympics in Paris. When Eric opens the letter with the scheduled sprints, to his great dismay, he is to run the 100-meter sprint on Sunday, July 6. Eric refuses, as he is convinced that God wants him to keep the Sabbath Day holy. There is a lot of pressure on him to conform to the expectation. "A traitor to Scottish sporting," proclaimed one paper. Finally, Eric entered 200 and 400 meter races which was not what he was the favourite in. Eric read the Scripture given to him by his coach before he ran, "For them that honour me I will honour."(1 Samuel 2:30). Against all odds, Eric won gold for England in the 400 m and broke the world record as he ran the sprint at 47.6 seconds.

There was another Olympic runner representing England, Harold Abrahams, who had become a friend of Eric. In the book Run to Glory, the two are running with two different motivations. Harold is a Jew and is feeling the anti-Semitic sentiments in Europe. He says, "If I could be the fastest man in the world," he thought," maybe then I would be treated like everyone else and granted the same level of respect."(pg. 64) Eric on the other hand, told his sister that God has made him fast and when he runs, he feels His pleasure. Eric was resting when he ran and he was resting when he rested, but Harold was always striving whether he rested or ran. There is a resting place in Jesus that the Bible refers to in Hebrews 4:9 there remains, then, a Sabbath-rest for the people of God; 10 for anyone who enters God's rest also rests from their works, just as God did from his. 11 Let us; therefore, make every effort to enter that rest."

No amount of good works can earn your heavenly Father's love and pleasure, only faith can. By faith in what Jesus has already done for you, you have access to all His promises; the greatest of these promises is adoption as a child of God. This faith is given to anyone who humbles themselves and repents for living a life apart from God's will, and who obeys His will in the Word of God. Jesus is that Sabbath rest that destroys all religion and who invites you to come as you are; dirty, sinful, guilty, and fearful.

So how do I live a life of rest? Jesus answered, "The work of God is this: to believe in the one he has sent." John 6: 29 I must do my part to be able to enter into rest and walk in His presence. Every morning I used to wake up thinking about all I must do, but now before I get out of bed, I praise Him and give thanks, worship Him and reflect on His Word. Worship reminds you who God is and who you are, and the Word teaches you what the Holy Spirit is saying for you to believe and to do. Also, I believe that corporate worship is essential. That is where we learn to love God together and learn to love each other. Remember, however, that rest comes from letting your Father hold you and whisper to you that you are His son or daughter with whom He is well pleased. Perfect love casts out all fear.

Why did Jesus create the Sabbath rest? What is the connection between the Gospel message and Sabbath rest? Why does religion not lead to rest? What area do you struggle with entering that rest?

Pray this out loud: Thank You, Jesus, for caring for my soul and body. Help me to understand how to apply the Sabbath rest, physically as well as spiritually. If there are areas in my soul where I don't trust You, but are darkened by striving and anxiety, show it to me that I might repent. Thank You for rest and peace that comes from Your presence.

5. The Word

Read the Gospel of Mark Chapter 4

Mark 4:9 Then Jesus said, "Whoever has ears to hear, let them hear." 10 When he was alone, the Twelve and the others around him asked him about the parables. 11 He told them, "The secret of the kingdom of God has been given to you. But to those on the outside everything is said in parables 12 so that they may be ever seeing but never perceiving, and ever hearing but never understanding; otherwise they might turn and be forgiven!"

Jesus is on a journey with the 12 disciples, making them into followers. He revealed Himself as the Anointed One (Christ), when He healed, drove out demons and forgave sins as if He was God. In addition, He declares Himself the Lord of the Sabbath. The question of who He is, is becoming clear. Now Jesus is ready to teach and reveal a key to becoming a follower of Jesus, especially to us who don't see Him in physical form.

Jesus tells the crowd a parable of a farmer scattering seeds. The seeds land on four different soils, the worn path, the rocky soil, the thorny soil and the good soil. After the parable He says nothing!

This is like a pastor I heard talking about his fiancée's grandfather. The grandfather, Carl, was a good storyteller, so one day he asked Shane, the pastor, "Have you heard the story of Anthony?" "Nope, don't recall that story." answered Shane.

"Well, let me tell you," the grandfather said. "Anthony was sitting at the old restaurant that used to be down the street from here having a coffee at the counter. One of the three Smitty boys came in; he had a pistol in his hand and shot Anthony point blank. He put the pistol on the counter and told the waitress to call the police."

That was it, no more story. Later that afternoon, he asked him for the meaning of that story since he couldn't see any connection. "Oh yeah," he said, "There's a connection. You are marrying my granddaughter and if you ever hurt her, then…! Get the point?" The disciples did not understand the parable either so a while later they asked Him, and this is how Jesus answered:

Mark 4:10 When he was alone, the Twelve and the others around him asked him about the parables. 11 He told them, "The secret of the kingdom of God has been given to you. But to those on the outside everything is said in parables 12 so that, they may be ever seeing but never perceiving, and ever hearing but never understanding; otherwise they might turn and be forgiven!"

Did you get this? Jesus told them that He gave the parable to confuse the crowd. Why? I was listening to Pastor Francis Chan, who gave me the answer, which was something like this: "If your grass seeds land on the sidewalk, why bother watering it?" Not everyone is able to accept or hear the Word at this point in their life, but some are. Jesus tells the disciples that the secret of the

Kingdom has been given to them.   He is saying that the hearts of the disciples are the good soil.

13 Then Jesus said to them, "Don't you understand this parable? How then will you understand any parable? 14 The farmer sows the word.15 Some people are like seed along the path, where the word is sown. As soon as they hear it, Satan comes and takes away the word that was sown in them. 16 Others, like seed sown on rocky places, hear the word and at once receive it with joy. 17 But since they have no root, they last only a short time. When trouble or persecution comes because of the word, they quickly fall away. 18 Still others, like seed sown among thorns, hear the word; 19 but the worries of this life, the deceitfulness of wealth and the desires for other things come in and choke the word, making it unfruitful. 20 Others, like seed sown on good soil, hear the word, accept it, and produce a crop—some thirty, some sixty, some a hundred times what was sown." (Mark 4)

What is the Word for Peter and the rest of the disciples? Is it the Bible? Yes, but it is it not just a word that is memorized or quoted, recited, or confessed, it is a living Word.   You cannot just take Scriptures as a lucky charm and expect the word to change your life.

Jesus made it clear to the Pharisees that even though they were studying the Scripture; they were missing the point of the Word. 39 You study[c] the Scriptures diligently because you think that in them you have eternal life. These are the very Scriptures that testify about me, 40 yet you refuse to come to me to have life. (John 5) Even the Old Testament was a Word that pointed to Jesus. For the word to be living, you need to read it as if Jesus is speaking to you.

The disciples did not have the New Testament, but they heard Jesus as He brought the truth. The word of God is not merely knowledge. The Bible is not a textbook; it is a book that will bring revelation to the heart if it is received with faith. Charles Spurgeon, one of the greatest preachers of the 19th century, heard the word as if for the first time when He sought shelter from a snowstorm in a Methodist church. Charles had felt that God was a mean taskmaster, not a loving God, but when he listened to the preacher, the truth came and broke open his heart. The preacher revealed the Gospel to Charles as he was speaking from Isaiah 45:22 "Turn to me and be saved, all you end of the earth; for I am God, and there is no other." You can look inside but there is no comfort there, only darkness. You need the light, the preacher said. On that snowy January day in 1850, the 15-year-old Charles became born again by a living Word. The Biography of Spurgeon by Arnold Dallimore (Moody Press, 1984), pages 18-20)

Peter thought of the Word as the Gospel, as shown in Mark 4:3 For you have been born again, not of perishable seed, but of imperishable, through the living and enduring word of God.24 For, "All people are like grass, and all their glory is like the flowers of the field; the grass withers and the flowers fall, 25 but the word of the Lord endures forever."And this is the word that was preached to you.

A seed is filled with potential to become what it was designed to be. If it is grass seed, it sprouts and becomes green grass begging to be cut. If it is a flower seed, under the right conditions, it grows until it blossoms. When the seed of God is planted in a heart, it grows under the right conditions to become what it was created to be, Christ likeness. Paul describes what that looks like in Galatians

5:22, "But the fruit of the Spirit is love, joy, peace, forbearance, kindness, goodness, faithfulness, 23 gentleness and self-control. Against such things there is no law. 24 Those who belong to Christ Jesus have crucified the flesh with its passions and desires."

As you notice, Paul calls the different attributes 'fruit', which is singular. By using fruit (singular), Paul is saying that the character traits are all connected as attributes of the one Spirit. You can be kind merely by personality or self will or fear; for example, a clerk might be kind and gentle in fear of losing her job, but she is not likely going to have joy. On the other hand, when someone like 'Son of Sam' who was a mass killer of women became a believer, his very character changed. Son of Sam, whose real name was David Richard Berkowitz, terrorized New York in 1976. He was eventually captured and given a 300-year prison sentence for six murders. A fellow prisoner led him to Jesus and the man who had once made a pact with the devil is now an aide to the chaplain in the prison. They say about him that he has a gentle spirit and his gentleness is very noticeable to others.

Remember the different soils are hearts. I asked the inmates at the women's prison what they thought the first example of the seeds landing on the path could mean. They answered, "It is like people with addictions who are not ready to surrender. They don't see their need to change." A hardened heart lacks humility and is not ready to hear. The message is quickly removed from their consciousness by the enemy, who whispers, "I don't need that, that is stupid. Look what you will have to give up." God opposes the proud but gives grace to the humble.

When the seeds land on the rocky soil, the heart receives it with joy. The person hears it and accepts the word, but eventually the person will encounter a test. One day I led a lady prisoner to Jesus, she was in a prison where a different spirituality was taught, so when inmates become Christians there is persecution. There is pressure to accept an alternative spirituality and if they don't, they will quickly feel ostracized and at times might lose privileges. One inmate told me one day, "I am tired of always being picked on because I am a Christian. I am ready to throw in the towel." She was doing the battle and fortunately she pulled through and has become a light for the Gospel. The residents will try to blend the two beliefs to be accepted. Who doesn't want to be loved and to fit in? Besides, we live in a culture that declares that tolerance is the highest value, an even more important value than truth. However, Jesus says, "I am the way... no other way leads to the Father." (John 14:6) There is only one way. The ones who give into the pressure eventually fall away. Over time, truth will clash with false beliefs and a choice will be made to either accept or reject. Unless the word has deep roots, the new believer will give into the culture around them and in their hearts will deny the truth. The heart might falsely conclude that all religion is good, or it might completely deny Jesus as God.

The other test or trial, for the second soil, is when bad things happen to you. Job lost everything and at one point his wife in desperation told him to curse God. Job 1:20 At this, Job got up and tore his robe and shaved his head. Then he fell to the ground in worship 21 and said:

50

"Naked I came from my mother's womb, and naked I will depart The Lord gave and the Lord has taken away; may the name of the Lord be praised."

Job even lost his health, yet he did not curse God. Job never knew why he suffered; in fact, he pleaded with God to give him an audience so he could defend himself, as if God blamed him for something. However, despite his desperate situation, he declared in Job 19:25, "I know that my redeemer lives, and that in the end he will stand on the earth."The temptation to give up when hardship comes your way is real and overcoming requires supernatural strength and faith. In Hudson Taylor's 51 years of ministry to the Chinese, he saw his house burn down, his stuff stolen, he was beaten, he went on 18 mission trips to the interior without seeing results. His medical supplies were stolen; he lost his wife and several children to disease. Yet he eventually had a breakthrough, baptizing over 50,000 people. What kept him from becoming bitter and resentful? It was that inner sense of a call or witness that he was indeed a son of God called to greatness, and the divine Holy Spirit convincing him that every promise was still available no matter the circumstances. (pg. 207 Roll Away Your Stone by Dutch Sheets)

The third heart is mentioned in Mark 4:18 "... like seed sown among thorns, hear the word; 19 but the worries of this life, the deceitfulness of wealth and the desires for other things come in and choke the word, making it unfruitful." We live in the most distracted and materialistic society ever. With more temptations at our fingertips than any generations before, and with a value system declaring that you deserve to be happy, this is probably the hardest to overcome for a modern-day new Christian. I just listened to a story by my friend Bob, who told me how shocked he was when he heard how a very close friend of his had left his wife and his faith. Bob and his wife had led worship with this guy. For years they went to the same church. This friend was frequently away from home on business trips. One day he told his wife that he had enough of Christianity and left her for another, leaving her and their kids devastated. Temptations are everywhere, so be on the alert. Check your heart; remember it is the wellspring of life. What is happening? Are your dreams and thoughts focused on worldly things or eternal things? If you went to court, would there be enough evidence, after checking your bank account and your whereabouts, to convict you of being a Christian?

The fourth heart hears the Word and gladly accepts it. How does a heart become fertile soil producing bumper crops? This is an abiding process, or as it is written in John 15: 4 "Remain in me, as I also remain in you. No branch can bear fruit by itself; it must remain in the vine. Neither can you bear fruit unless you remain in me." This process begins with hearing the Word. You hear it by either the spoken Word or the written Word. In either case, you receive it as if God is speaking to you personally. Secondly, the Word is like the child in the womb of a mother, it takes nine months before it is ready to be born. After meditating on it, worshipping with it, praying it and declaring it, the Word will lead to revelation. The truth becomes a reality in the heart. Finally, it needs to be accepted. According to Dutch Sheets that means it needs to be obeyed. When the Bible says to forgive, you forgive. (See Roll Away Your Stone, by Dutch Sheets page 232.) When it says to love your enemies, you do return good to those who hate you. When it says to give, you give. When it says to pray, you pray. When it says to go and make disciples, you look for a way to plug in and see that commandment come through.

We might frequently go through a process where we start with a hardened heart, but through the work of the Spirit the heart becomes softer and ends up being the good soil. I just had lunch with a journalist whose heart is being softened by the Holy Spirit. He had grown up as a Catholic, but he did not believe that Jesus is God. He had plenty of religious background, but he had no encounter. I knew he was interested in Alexander Solzhenitsyn, who is famous for his writing about the Communist prison systems in his book called The Gulag Archipelago, which is about the Soviet prison system during the Stalin regime. I had read his conversion story written by Chuck Colson in his book, Loving God, chapter 2.

Chuck tells the story of a Jewish doctor, Boris Kornfield, who had become a political prisoner in Siberia in the 1950. Boris had looked to Communism for salvation, but probably in seeing the abuse of power, had turned against communism. As an atheist he encountered a Christian in the same prison who spoke of a Jewish Messiah. The Christian frequently quoted the Lord's Prayer. Chuck Colson speculates that his heart was probably exposed when one day he was faced with having to do surgery on a hated guard. Boris remembered the words repeated to him by his Christian friend, "Forgive me for my sin as I forgive those who sin against me." How could Boris forgive? He wanted to hate and kill him. Was he any different from the guard? Boris let him live because Jesus had forgiven him at the cross of Calvary. One night, Boris was performing a surgery on a patient with intestinal cancer. After the surgery, Boris began to tell his patient how he had experienced peace. Boris confessed that we all deserved punishment for our sins: "I have become convinced that there is no punishment that comes to us in this life on earth which is undeserved." I do not know how he ended his testimony, but it would have led to the truth that Jesus took that punishment that we deserved upon Himself. Jesus died a death that we should have died. The patient awoke the next morning to the running footsteps of people who had just discovered a man beaten to death by a mallet. The doctor had been killed in the night, but the patient remembered his words and pondered them until he also turned from one Jew, Karl Marx as his saviour, to another Jew, Jesus Christ as the Saviour of his soul. The patient's name was Alexander Solzhenitsyn. Alexander was a Jew who had become atheist under the communist revolution. However, just like Boris, Alexander had seen the ugly face of communism and wanted nothing to do with it. What softened his heart was that he survived a surgery that normally was a death sentence. A surgery in a Siberian prison with its lack of medicine and equipment usually meant death. That he survived was a miracle. Alexander had also heard the confession of faith of another Jew on what might have felt like his deathbed. The good soil is a heart that hears the Word. Those words led him to faith. Boris himself had a hardened heart but through the circumstance of prison stripping him of all that he had, he heard the Word of Jesus through a Christian who repeated the Lord's Prayer to him. Those words opened his heart to his own sinfulness. No longer could he just blame Stalin and the guards. He needed forgiveness. Frequently, Jesus will use circumstances to help you hear the Word of life. I grew up in Denmark and was inundated with atheism. I could not hear God until he planted me in the hills near Maple Creek, Canada. After I had pursued everything that I thought could bring meaning and significance, like a career, a family and building a house, I knew that there was more. This hunger for more opened my spirit to hear what the Spirit of the Lord said.

Luke 8: 14 The seed that fell among thorns stands for those who hear, but as they go on their way they are choked by life's worries, riches and pleasures, and they do not mature."

James 1: 22 "Do not merely listen to the word, and so deceive yourselves. Do what it says. 23 Anyone who listens to the word but does not do what it says is like someone who looks at his face in a mirror 24 and, after looking at himself, goes away and immediately forgets what he looks like. 25 But whoever looks intently into the perfect law that gives freedom and continues in it—not forgetting what they have heard but doing it—they will be blessed in what they do." 2 Peter 1: 4 "Through these he has given us his very great and precious promises, so that through them you may participate in the divine nature, having escaped the corruption in the world caused by evil desires."

Hebrews 412 "For the word of God is alive and active. Sharper than any double-edged sword, it penetrates even to dividing soul and spirit, joints and marrow; it judges the thoughts and attitudes of the heart. 13 Nothing in all creation is hidden from God's sight. Everything is uncovered and laid bare before the eyes of him to whom we must give account."

John 8: 31 "To the Jews who had believed him, Jesus said, "If you hold to my teaching, you are really my disciples. 32 Then you will know the truth, and the truth will set you free."

John 5:24 "Very truly I tell you, whoever hears my word and believes him who sent me has eternal life and will not be judged but has crossed over from death to life."

The Word is alive. In what way has the Word been alive to you?

What are some Scriptures that have brought about change in your life?

Would you consider your heart to be fertile soil? Why or why not?

Pray: Dear Jesus, help me to have a heart that is pliable and tender towards Your leading. Help me, Lord, to take responsibility for what I am in control of, and to let go of what I cannot change.

6. Jesus in the Storm

Read the Gospel of Mark Chapter 8

The disciples are on a journey of discovery. Who is this Jesus? Jesus demonstrates His authority in his teachings as if His words were God's. Jesus takes authority over sickness and demons. He forgives sin as if all sin was done against Him, as if He is God. Jesus declares that He is Lord of the Sabbath, which is the same thing as saying that He wrote it. Then Jesus gives a teaching on the power of the Word to multiply; that is, if it lands in the right heart of faith and humility and acceptance.

Followers of Jesus, listen up, today's lesson must be learned on the job. Jesus will show us what can happen when we set out with Him in obedience to his calling. We will experience opposition.

35 That day when evening came, he said to his disciples, "Let us go over to the other side." 36 Leaving the crowd behind, they took him along, just as he was, in the boat. There were also other boats with him. 37 A furious squall came up, and the waves broke over the boat, so that it was nearly swamped. 38 Jesus was in the stern,

sleeping on a cushion. The disciples woke him and said to him, "Teacher, don't you care if we drown?"

39 He got up, rebuked the wind and said to the waves, "Quiet! Be still!" Then the wind died down and it was completely calm. 40 He said to his disciples, "Why are you so afraid? Do you still have no faith?" 41 They were terrified and asked each other, "Who is this? Even the wind and the waves obey him!"(Mark 4)

There are many storms, and some are self-made. Because of my sin I have gotten myself into trouble. Samson lost his strength and freedom as lust led him into the bed of Delilah, who subsequently betrayed him for money. Other storms are circumstantial, like health, financial or relational. The doctor gives you a bad report. Your wife leaves you a note of goodbye. Your son is in jail. Other storms might be caused by God to bring correction, like when Jonah ran away from God and as he was heading in the opposite way of God's direction, God sent a storm. Finally, there is a storm caused by the enemy who wants to stop you from getting you to where God wants you to be. Satan wants to stop you from reaching your destination. This last example is what we have here in Mark 4. However; whatever storm you are in, you can have Jesus with you -- something that is highly recommended!

The disciples are at the center of God's will. This storm is not caused by their disobedience; they are victims of a storm. The storm wants to stop them from their destiny, which is the other side of the Sea of Galilee. Where is their beloved Messiah? He is sleeping and more specifically, He is sleeping in the stern on a pillow. (You may ask why all these details? One reason for the details is because you are reading an eyewitness account.) I was asked the other day at the Bible study at the prison why Jesus was sleeping. The most spiritual answer I could think of is that He was very tired. Sailing through 10-20-foot waves while sleeping either means that you are very tired or you are napping with one eye open watching to see what the disciples were going to do about it. The Sea of Galilee is 700 feet below sea level and the nearby Mount Hermon, 38 miles from the large lake, is 9000 feet above sea level. When the cold air from the mountain meets the warm air from the Sea of Galilee, you have a storm. This was such a bad storm that it caused panic in the seasoned fishermen who would have experienced many storms in their lives. They thought they were going to die.

The problem with a storm is that you cannot see very well, and so you imagine the worst, you question things and you embrace fear, not faith. I know from experience. Like I heard T.D Jakes say (or rather yell), pretending to be Job: "I cannot see God, He is not to the right, He is not to the left, He is not behind me. You were supposed to keep my back. You are not in front of me. You are supposed to lead me. I cannot see you."   In the storm you cannot see; that is why God says that we do not live by sight, but we live by faith. We do not live by what is visible, but we live by what is invisible, because the visible is temporary, but the invisible is eternal.

In the storm, there is the problem of the outward elements that might kill you physically, but what kills you spiritually is when the storm moves on the inside. The disciples panicked and as they woke Jesus up, they cried, "Don't you even care that we are going to drown?" There is the Problem of the wind and the waves, or the cancer and the bankruptcy, or the divorce and the loss of job. Nevertheless, when your anxiety begins to question the goodness of

God, you are inviting in a storm that is empowered by Satan, preventing you from your destiny. The sign of the internal struggle is when you blame others and especially blame God's heart for not caring. But when we see no way out then it often feels like God does not care, which leads us to the question of how to overcome the storm.

Yes, Jesus was probably tired, but He also had an internal peace that allowed Him to rest even in the middle of a storm. When He rebuked the disciples for their lack of faith, it was because He expected them to have the same peace. Jesus spoke to the storm out of peace. If you are anxious and fearful, you might cry out all you want, but you will have no power over the storm. There is a peace available to us in the storm anchored in the fact that when Jesus is in the boat, you will arrive on the other side.

Peter was as much in panic as the other ones and would probably have run off if it were not that he was in a boat in the middle of a sea with nowhere to go. Peter later learned how to live out of peace. In Acts 12, Peter is in prison. Herod had already executed James and was just waiting for an opportunity to kill Peter. This is what it says: Acts 12:6 "The night before Herod was to bring him to trial, Peter was sleeping between two soldiers, bound with two chains, and sentries stood guard at the entrance. 7 Suddenly an angel of the Lord appeared, and a light shone in the cell. He struck Peter on the side and woke him up. "Quick, get up!" he said, and the chains fell off Peter's wrists." Peter was facing execution and he knew it, yet he was in deep sleep when the angel woke him up.

Peter had received the peace of God. In His departing words, Jesus told the disciples: "27 Peace I leave with you; my peace I give you. I do not give to you as the world gives. Do not let your hearts be troubled and do not be afraid."(John 14:27) Peter knew that if he was executed then he would be in another place with Jesus and indeed he would be better off; if not, then Jesus had more for him to do and a miracle would be forthcoming.

I was listening to an interview with Rev. Jentezen Franklin, who spoke about fear. He shared his testimony of when he and his family once were on a plane when the co-pilot came into the passenger compartment with a mask on and declared that they needed to do an emergency landing.   A few minutes later the masks descended from the ceiling and they began to smell smoke. The interviewer asked Jentezen what was going through his mind at this moment. His answer was something like this, "We were just coming off a 21-day fast and I had a meal in front me. I looked at the meal and I thought I better eat that first."   Jentezen had an inner peace that kept him from panic.

When I heard that story, I thought of David in Psalm 23:4... "Even though I walk through the darkest valley, I will fear no evil, for you are with me; your rod and your staff, they comfort me. 5 You prepare a table before me in the presence of my enemies." Where is God? He is "with me" declares David! Where is God in your life? When Joshua faced fear, God said in Joshua 1:9 "Have I not commanded you? Be strong and courageous. Do not be afraid; do not be discouraged, for the Lord your God will be with you wherever you go." He told the disciples in Matthew 28:20: "And surely, I am with you always, to the very end of the age." The peace comes from that inner assurance that God is in you and with you.

The rod and the staff that bring comfort in the middle of the storm are His Word. When it seems like all hell is breaking loose, find a Word. Here is one from Isaiah 43:2 "When you pass through the waters, I will be with you." One day not long ago I was very discouraged and as I was reading my Bible, I came across this word in 2 Chronicles 20:15, "This is what the Lord says to you: 'Do not be afraid or discouraged because of this vast army, for the battle is not yours but God's." I felt this was God speaking to me and I rejoiced.

One day I did a funeral, and at the tea, a man with broken English came and introduced himself to me as Sunol. He told me that his wife was not a believer and so when I preached about eternal life, he tapped his wife with an elbow, whispering in her ear, "Listen to what he says, there is eternal life." I was curious so I asked him where he came from. He told me Turkey, and then proceeded to tell me that he was Muslim. I asked him what he believed, and he told me that he (like me) believed in a God and that some day we would die and hopefully would go into heaven if we have done enough good things. I told him that is where we differ. Through Jesus, I have my assurance of salvation and heaven. This assurance does not come because of my good works, but because of what He did for me. My part is to humble myself, receive the good news by faith, and live it out. My newfound Muslim friend does not have peace and will never know how much he must 'do' before God will accept his works as the wages for salvation.

I heard an interview about Joni Erickson Tada. When she was a young lady, she had everything going for her. She was beautiful, smart, athletic and a gifted painter. She was a Christian, but a lukewarm believer. Then one day all her dreams vanished because of one devastating accident. She jumped into a lake that was too shallow, broke her neck and subsequently became a quadriplegic. Everything from her neck down was numb. Little by little, through the help of a Christian friend, she regained her hope in a good God and she discovered her mission in life. Through her books, her radio program and her ministry to the handicapped, she has touched millions with the Gospel. Recently she was diagnosed with breast cancer. The interviewer asked if she was discouraged. She answered by saying something like this, "Oh no! God is up to something great and the enemy is trying to stop me. When I go for my treatments, I use every opportunity to speak to the other patients about the hope I have in Jesus." She quoted the Scripture, "But my righteous one will live by faith. And I take no pleasure in the one who shrinks back." Hebrews 10:38

Have you ever been in a storm? How did you react?

What was Jesus expecting of the disciples when He asked, "Do you still have no faith?"

How do we wake up Jesus in our storm?

Pray: Dear Jesus, I am drowning as I am facing the impossible. You can silence the storm. Will You give me hope, a promise a word an encouragement? I thank You Jesus that You are the God of the impossible. You can do even more than I can imagine or think. I thank You, Jesus that I can do all things through Christ who strengthens me.

7. Who touched me?

Read the Gospel of Mark Chapter 7

Mark 5:21 "When Jesus had again crossed over by boat to the other side of the lake, a large crowd gathered around him while he was by the lake.22 Then one of the synagogue leaders, named Jairus, came, and when he saw Jesus, he fell at his feet. 23 He pleaded earnestly with him, "My little daughter is dying. Please come and put your hands on her so that she will be healed and live." 24 So Jesus went with him.

A large crowd followed and pressed around him. 25 And a woman was there who had been subject to bleeding for twelve years. 26 She had suffered a great deal under the care of many doctors and had spent all she had, yet instead of getting better, she grew worse. 27 When she heard about Jesus, she came up behind him in the crowd and touched his cloak, 28 because she thought, "If I just touch his clothes, I will be healed." 29 Immediately her bleeding stopped and she felt in her body that she was freed from her suffering.

30 At once Jesus realized that power had gone out from him. He turned around in the crowd and asked, "Who touched my clothes?" 31 "You see the people crowding against you," his disciples answered, "and yet you can ask, 'Who touched me?'"

32 But Jesus kept looking around to see who had done it. 33 Then the woman, knowing what had happened to her, came and fell at his feet and, trembling with fear, told him the whole truth. 34 He said to her, "Daughter, your faith has healed you. Go in peace and be freed from your suffering." 35 While Jesus was still speaking, some people came from the house of Jairus, the synagogue leader. "Your daughter is dead," they said. "Why bother the teacher anymore?" 36 Overhearing what they said, Jesus told him, "Don't be afraid; just believe." 37 He did not let anyone follow him except Peter, James and John the brother of James. 38 When they came to the home of the synagogue leader, Jesus saw a commotion, with people crying and wailing loudly.39 He went in and said to them, "Why all this commotion and wailing? The child is not dead but asleep." 40 But they laughed at him.

After he put them all out, he took the child's father and mother and the disciples who were with him and went in where the child was.41 He took her by the hand and said to her, "Talitha koum!" (which means "Little girl, I say to you, get up!"). 42 Immediately the girl stood up and began to walk around (she was twelve years old). At this they were completely astonished. 43 He gave strict orders not to let anyone know about this and told them to give her something to eat."

Have you ever been desperate for a breakthrough? Once when I was heading to my father's funeral in Denmark, I ended up in an airport outside London an hour too late for my plane. Great, what do I do now? This was before cell phones. I had one of the airport employees leave a message at the Danish airport that I wasn't going to make it. I went to the airline to see if there was another flight that night. There was a plane, but it was filled up and there were five people on the waiting list, and I could be number six for $300.00, which meant that it was highly unlikely that I would get on the plane. I thought I could stay overnight and go the next day as this was Thursday and the funeral wasn't until Saturday. Just as I was about to fall asleep on my chair, I heard my name being called. My sister was on the phone telling me that I had to come that day because the funeral had been changed to Friday at ten in the morning. What do I do? I prayed, "Lord, if You want me to be there for the funeral You have to get me there especially since You gave me something to say at my dad's funeral." I decided to check if there was another airline, and there was. They had one ticket left for Copenhagen, which is about a two-hour train ride from where I needed to be.   I bought it and landed in Copenhagen at midnight. I asked when the last train was for the night and was told, "It is right now, if you run down those stairs you might make it."I made it at two in the morning.   How did I get my breakthrough? I prayed. I got up from my chair expecting that God would help me.

Like any good father would feel, Jairus felt desperate for a miracle. He felt so desperate that he was willing to humble himself and go against his own doctrine. Jairus was a religious ruler and that meant most likely a Pharisee whose religion saw Jesus as an imposter. However, Jairus had heard about Jesus doing miracles and so he went looking for him. This might have cost him his job, but he didn't care.   He found Jesus and fell at His feet. The Word promises, "Humble yourselves, therefore, under God's mighty hand, that he may lift you up in due time." (1 Peter 5:6) Jairus did just that, humbled himself. As a religious ruler, he would have been a man of influence and wealth; still he bowed his knees before Jesus, whom the Pharisees saw as an enemy. If you want a breakthrough, you must let go of your pride.

Jesus hears about Jairus' daughter and decides to go with him. When you pray, God hears your need. Here is the sequence of the journey of breakthrough: problem, promise and provision. However, as you will see, frequently a testing precedes the provision. Jairus presented the problem. Jesus promised to go with him, but then came the testing. Jairus is anxious and in a hurry, his daughter is dying. Jesus suddenly stopped and asked, "Who touched me?" When an answer does not come the way you expected or as fast as you thought you needed it, there is a crisis of faith. Jesus stopped. Doesn't He know that a girl is dying?

A woman with an illness causing bleeding had touched Jesus. The woman had suffered for twelve years not only from her illness, but also from the many doctors whom she had tried and spent all her money. The Jewish law demanded that women who were bleeding should be in isolation and not touch anyone in case they contaminated others. But this woman overcame the fear of being arrested as she sneaked in among the crowd to touch the only one who could possibly heal her. "If only I can do it anonymously, no one would know," she probably thought.

Many times, we wish that our dealing with God could just be private; no need to bow our knees in front of people, no need to go to church, no need for anyone to know; that way you couldn't be accused of being a fanatical Bible thumper. I have heard it said that when you come to Jesus you tend to receive more than you expect, and you tend to give more than you intend.

This was certainly the case for this woman. She realized that she was, as my grandson would say, "Busted!" In shame and fear, she confessed what had just happened. Jesus did not reprimand her or criticize her, but He honoured her and said, "Your faith has healed you." Jesus was impressed with her faith. There is one thing that impresses God and that is faith. (see Matthew 8:10)

Her faith came from hearing about Jesus; Jairus' faith would also have come through hearing, and so did yours. Romans 10:17 "Consequently, faith comes from hearing the message, and the message is heard through the word about Christ." However, James declares that faith without action is dead; therefore, a breakthrough frequently requires an action.

Moses had to lift the rod to part the sea, Joshua had to walk around Jericho, Naaman had to dip in the river seven times for his leprosy to be healed. David had to find a stone and sling it. The disciples had to wait in the upper room. The woman did not just pray, she went to where she could find Jesus, and the Holy Spirit anointing flowed through Him into her. Jairus not only prayed; he went to find Jesus. The breakthrough requires not only faith but also an action. Breakthrough involves prayer, perseverance and participation as your faith is tested. There is a problem, there is a promise and there is provision. But before the provision there is a test.

Hannah pleaded with God for a son. Year after year, she went to the temple to pray. She told God that if He would give her a son, she would dedicate him to His service as a priest. There is something about fasting and pleading with God that brings a breakthrough.

Here is a parable of Jesus in Luke 18:1, "Then Jesus told his disciples a parable to show them that they should always pray and not give up. 2 He said: "In a certain town there was a judge who neither feared God nor cared what people thought.3 And there was a widow in that town who kept coming to him with the plea, 'Grant me justice against my adversary.'

4 "For some time he refused. But finally, he said to himself, 'Even though I don't fear God or care what people think, 5 yet because this widow keeps bothering me, I will see that she gets justice, so that she won't eventually come and attack me!'"

6 And the Lord said, "Listen to what the unjust judge says. 7 And will not God bring about justice for his chosen ones, who cry out to him day and night? Will he keep putting them off? 8 I tell you, he will see that they get justice, and quickly. However, when the Son of Man comes, will he find faith on the earth?"

Are you in need of a breakthrough right now? What is it?

Are you going through a test of faith? Can you identify with Hannah?

Pray: Dear Jesus, I need faith to endure my trial, so please help me. I pray for a breakthrough in this area _____. Thank You, Jesus that You hear me.

8. Who is this Jesus?

Read the Gospel of Mark Chapter 8

Who feeds the thousands and walks on water?

Mark6:48 "He saw the disciples straining at the oars, because the wind was against them. Shortly before dawn he went out to them, walking on the lake. He was about to pass by them, 49 but when they saw him walking on the lake, they thought he was a ghost. They cried out, 50 because they all saw him and were terrified.

Immediately he spoke to them and said, "Take courage! It is I. Do not be afraid." 51 Then he climbed into the boat with them, and the wind died down. They were completely amazed, 52 for they had not understood about the loaves; their hearts were hardened."

Remember Jesus is taking the disciples on a journey of discovering who He is, who they are and what they are called to do. As a good teacher, He teaches, demonstrates and then sends them out two by two. Soon, however, they are not going to have Him in physical form, so how are they going to overcome storms and insurmountable needs as they step out to disciple the world? Jesus is about to teach them.

A large group of people is following Jesus and He feels compassion for them. They are spiritually lost. He begins to teach them.   The hours go by and no one is moving.   The sun is descending over the horizon and Jesus is not stopping. I suspect however, that the disciples are getting hungry, and that is the real reason why they suggest to Jesus that He dismisses them to go and find food. Jesus responds by telling them to feed the people. They could only see what they did not have, so they respond with saying that that will take a whole year's wages. What is worth noticing is that the people did not move. They were hungry for the Word and would rather have the Word than food.   Could it be true that when there is a hunger for the Word, there is also provision for physical needs? Hebrews 11:6 declares: "...he rewards those who earnestly seek him."

I was just reading a book called An Asian Harvest by Paul Hathaway. He grew up in New Zealand and as a teen he dropped out of school and went to Australia to find a job.   Finally, he got a job in a factory.   There was a friend Danny who invited Paul to church.   Paul laughed and told him he would come and laugh at him and his church. But since this was his only real friend, he decided to go along.   Paul felt the sermon was directed towards him when the pastor quoted this passage out of 2 Timothy 3:1 "But mark this: There will be terrible times in the last days. 2 People will be lovers of themselves, lovers of money, boastful, proud, abusive, disobedient to their parents, ungrateful, unholy, 3 without love, unforgiving, slanderous, without self-control, brutal, not lovers of the good, 4 treacherous, rash, conceited, lovers of pleasure rather than lovers of God—"

Paul gave his heart to Jesus that night. The result was a hunger for the Word. Paul read the Bible every moment he could. As he was reading it, he discovered the truth that Jesus was the only way to heaven, there were not multiple ways. Within the next month, Paul heard two missionaries from China sharing their stories in the local church. One of them had been in prison for over 20 years for preaching the gospel. This man was now a leader of thousands of underground cell churches. The missionary asked if anyone wanted to be a donkey for Jesus; that is, be willing to smuggle Bibles into China. Paul instantly thought this was what God called him to do, so he signed up, even though he was newly saved and had no money.

Paul had a conviction one night that Jesus would provide for him. He was given Matthew 6:31 "So do not worry, saying, 'What shall we eat?' or 'What shall we drink?' or 'What shall we wear?' 32 For the pagans run after all these things and your heavenly Father knows that you need them. 33 But seek first his kingdom and his righteousness and all these things will be given to you as well." Paul hung onto this promise. He knew he needed money for airfare to Hong Kong and he needed money to stay at the mission base, but he had no money. The next day, after having this conviction that God will be his provider, his uncle woke him up and gave him an envelope. He told Paul that God had told him to give him $750. Paul shared with us readers how he had made a commitment to go to Hong Kong to smuggle Bibles and he needed that exact amount for an airfare. This was the beginning of Paul's lifelong ministry called Asian Harvest. They no longer smuggle

Bibles into China; they illegally print them and distribute them within the country. By 2016 they had distributed over ten million bibles. They figured that for every Bible given, three people would be saved. Paul, together with his team, are believing for $40 million to print 20 million Bibles to send to many Asian countries.

Paul shares many stories of how the Chinese (like the people listening to Jesus) are hungry for the Word. They would sit from 7 in the morning until supper just listening. When the Bibles arrived in those remote rural areas by courageous couriers, the underground church celebrated as if the greatest gift was given to them. These Christian brothers risked torture and imprisonment because of their commitment to the Word. We can hardly get out of bed on Sunday morning to listen to a half-hour sermon expounding on the Word. Given the choice between food and the Word, they would take the Word.

Just like the disciples, Paul had to learn that God was their provider. Jesus sent out the disciples without any earthly belongings but with a promise that He would be with them. The multiplication of bread was a demonstration of what Jesus can do even with only two fish and five loaves.

One of the spiritual principles of miracles of provision is thankfulness. Look at what you have with thankfulness -- in this case two loaves and five fish. Jesus starts with what you have. Tell him with thankfulness and tell Him you are willing to let it go. Do not look at what you do not have. Do not focus on your lack; focus on what you have and what you can give. You might not be happy be with your house, but praise God you have a house. You might not like your car, but praise God for wheels. Are you ready to change focus? The disciples could only see what they didn't have, a years' wages to pay for bread.

2 Cor. 9: 10 Now he who supplies seed to the sower and bread for food will also supply and increase your store of seed and will enlarge the harvest of your righteousness. 11 You will be enriched in every way so that you can be generous on every occasion, and through us your generosity will result in thanksgiving to God." Everything we have are like seeds; we can sow it into God's Kingdom and expect a harvest. As we sow, God will increase the seeds. Paul gave everything he had, and he trusted God for provision. This arrangement led Paul to be an instrument of God delivering millions of Bibles. This arrangement led the disciples to be instruments of God changing the world.

The second spiritual principle is the breaking of bread. Before the miracle comes, there is often a breaking of your will and agenda and pride. Jesus takes the bread and the fish, and He breaks them and gives thanks as He looks to heaven. Whenever you find a powerful woman or man mightily used by God, you find someone who has been broken.

In 1994, I met my friend John Kpewoan. He was a refugee from Liberia, where a civil war had broken out. They had lined him up to shoot him, but before his turn came, some stranger with authority stepped in and said, "Let him go." John escaped and ended up among 250,000 refugees in Sierra Leone, where he contacted cholera. The doctor had diagnosed his disease as fatal, but by the grace of God he survived. From there he ended up in South Africa, where the UN gave him a ticket to Regina. In the winter of 1994, I met him at our church. We became friends and I discovered that his vision was to go back and start an orphanage.

In year 2000, he went back and bought 8 acres. He then built an orphanage for 70 children and a school for between 350 to 500 students.

John was broken through a civil war crisis, where he learned that God is His shield and protector and healer. When he started the orphanage, he had to learn to start with being thankful for what little he had and ask God for a continued miracle of provision to sponsor the students. The orphan compound exists because John heard the call and because God heard the cry of His people in Liberia. The Asian Harvest exists because God heard the cry of His people in China for Bibles and because Paul heard the call. The disciples were going to be sent out with little earthly goods but the clothes on their backs. They were going to turn the world upside down. But for now, they didn't understand the lesson of the bread. They were not ready.

When Moses met God in the wilderness at the burning bush, he too faced the impossible and needed to learn who this Elohim is. Elohim is Hebrew for God almighty. This is my paraphrase from Exodus 3: God told Moses that He had heard the cry of His enslaved people in Egypt and He was now sending Moses. Moses was very reluctant and afraid of going back to where he was accused of murder. So, Moses asked who shall I say who You are? God answered with these famous words, "I am who I am." I can just see Moses thinking, "That is great, but send someone else." Like Moses, we don't fully understand who this is calling us.

Moses led the former slaves into the wilderness and there came the test; how do you feed a million and half people where there is nothing but sand. Moses had a desperate prayer, "If you do not come through, we will starve, and your name will be ridiculed." We need a similar cry, "If you don't come through, Lord, Your church will not be able to pass on the light to the next generation." The world around us is dying of spiritual starvation. We have more Bibles and teaching materials than ever, but we have very few radical disciples.

Who is this Jesus who calms the storm and feeds the thousands? When the disciples saw Jesus walking on the water in a storm, they had forgotten how He had just fed the thousands. If Jesus can feed the thousands, can He not also walk on water and calm the storm? The past miracles are supposed to give us faith for the next storm, or next crisis of needs. The Hebrew slaves were supposed to have received their faith through the desert as God provided and protected them, but when they faced the giants, they could only see what they didn't have. They had forgotten God's miracles. Have you forgotten?

One of the principles of God's provision is faith. Has God given you a Scripture of promise for provision? Another principle for supernatural provision is thankfulness. Can you give thanks for His provision? Another principle of supernatural provision is giving. This is a sowing and reaping principle. Are you ready to tithe?

Pray: Dear Jesus, give me a promise of provision and show me how I can be part of the sowing and reaping principle. How do You want me to spend my money?

9. What Is IN Your heart?

Read the Gospel of Mark Chapter 9

Why was Jesus a bit of a scrapper, especially when it came to the Pharisees?   He would frequently break their rules and tell them something about their hearts, like calling them whitewashed tombs.   Clean on the outside, but dead on the inside. I believe the reason Jesus confronts the Pharisees is to expose their hearts.   The Pharisees sent someone to examine Jesus to see if He followed the rules. And this is what they said in Mark 7:5 "So the Pharisees and teachers of the law asked Jesus, "Why don't your disciples live according to the tradition of the elders instead of eating their food with defiled hands?"

The Pharisees demanded that people washed their hands and the dishes before they ate, not because of hygiene, but as a spiritual cleansing. Jesus answered by pointing out what needs to change in a man.   Mark 7:6 "He replied, "Isaiah was right when he prophesied about you hypocrites; as it is written:

"'These people honour me with their lips, but their hearts are far from me.

7 They worship me in vain; their teachings are merely human rules.' 8 You have let go of the commands of God and are holding on to human traditions.".... Mark 7:20 He went on: "What comes out of a person is what defiles them.21 For it is from within, out of a person's heart, that evil thoughts come—sexual immorality, theft, murder, 22 adultery, greed, malice, deceit, lewdness, envy, slander, arrogance and folly. 23 All these evils come from inside and defile a person."

Jesus points out how He wants a heart of worship. Sometimes I hug my wife while thinking of something else, and she will say, "Where are you?" Or I will sit and listen while thinking about my sermon, and she may feel, "You are not even listening. You don't care about me." That is what Jesus is saying when He says that we honour Him with our lips, but our hearts are far from Him. But what does the Bible mean when it talks about our hearts?

Tim Keller shares about how we pin emotions against thoughts, feelings against the mind. In the age of reason, emotions and passion were considered unworthy, equal to animal instinct, and needed to be crushed or ignored. Your ability to think is what made you who you are. Today, our culture also pins the two against each other, except now it is your passion that makes you who you are, not your reason. The modern-day advice is to look inside and discover your passion and dreams and pursue them, and let no one stop you. The Bible's understanding of the heart is very different. The heart is the seat of what you really believe. What you really believe will influence both your thoughts and your feelings. What you really believe is not necessarily the same as what you say you believe. What you really believe in your heart is what you eventually express in your behaviour. The Bible declares that we are to love God with all our hearts, that we are to trust Him with all our hearts, that where our treasure is, that is where our heart is, and that we are to guard our heart because it is the wellspring of life.

Jonathon Edwards says that we might have a sense of what is right, but we don't know it until we begin to live accordingly. I had started smoking when I was 14 even though my health teacher warned us with films of people dying from lung cancer. At 21, I arrived in Canada and met my wife, who hated smoking. If someone had asked me if I knew that smoking was bad for my health, I would have said yes. However, one day my wife took me to a couple of her former landlords where she had boarded as a student. The man had emphysema. He could barely breathe, yet in his hand he held a can of home-rolled cigarettes. I told myself, "If I don't stop it, I will look like him in a few years." I went outside and broke my pipe. That moment in that house was when I knew that smoking was bad for me. Before then my heart didn't really know.

Many times, we don' actually know what is in our hearts until tested. For example, Peter thought that he had the ability to give his heart fully to Jesus even unto death. This is what is recorded in John 13: 37 Peter asked, "Lord, why can't I follow you now? I will lay down my life for you." 38 Then Jesus answered, "Will you really lay down your life for me? Very truly I tell you, before the rooster crows, you will disown me three times!"

Jesus revealed Peter's heart at a time when even Peter didn't know His own heart. Trials and difficulties often reveal what is buried beneath the surface.

It is not what you say, but what you do that will reveal your heart. I was with a friend the other day who was going through a divorce. He was telling me about a Bible study he was leading on forgiveness, and how some of the group members were unwilling to acknowledge their own unforgiveness. This very friend had just been telling me about how bad his wife had treated him. He couldn't see his own unforgiveness.

The church I am pastoring now had split seven years before I arrived. The pastor of the split church came every Tuesday morning to pray with me. And I dreaded it. He always came bragging about what God did on the previous Sunday. I was angry at God, "Why did you call me to this church, when you do everything down the street and not here?" As clear as what seemed like an audible voice, I remember God answering me. "Why are you looking down the street? I did not call you there." My heart was jealous, and God corrected me.

King David knew what was in his heart and when he tried to hide it, God deliberately exposed his sin. (2 Samuel 12) King David's heart lusted for Bathsheba, and he got her pregnant. To cover his sin, he arranged for her husband to be killed. God sent the prophet Nathan to expose his crime. King David repented and wrote Psalm 51. David committed adultery, lied and killed. How bad can it get? Yet God forgave him.

One of the ways to connect your heart with Jesus is to be transparent. When it comes to the sins of our hearts, we are given a promise in 1 John 1:9 "If we confess our sins, he is faithful and just and will forgive us our sins and purify us from all unrighteousness."

King David gives a great example of opening his heart to God. In Psalm 51, we see David's prayer: "Cleanse me with hyssop, and I will be clean; wash me, and I will be whiter than snow. 8 Let me hear joy and gladness; let the bones you have crushed rejoice. 9 Hide your face from my sins and blot out all my iniquity. 10 Create in me a pure heart, O God, and renew a steadfast spirit within me."

Ask the Lord to examine your heart. Emotions are an indicator of what is going on in the heart. If you experience jealousy or anger, ask Jesus where it is coming from.

Often the way we see others and ourselves has to do with a belief system in our hearts. For example, if you look down upon people who are messier than you, is it because your value is tied to how neat and tidy you keep things? Where did that value come from? I valued educated and intelligent people because that is what my father with a great 8 education valued. Your heart contains your value system, and it may or may not be the value system of Jesus.

Pray:

Dear Jesus, show me my heart. Are there any evil thoughts or emotions keeping me in captivity? I choose to forgive _____ (name) who has hurt me or offended me. I confess anything I have done to hurt others and myself. I ask that You forgive me and cleanse me. Create in me a clean heart.

10. Who is qualified to be at your table?

Read the Gospel of Mark Chapter 10.

I want to share the story of the Syrophoenician woman who shows up in Mark chapter 7. To understand the story, you need to understand the Jewish religious culture. The Jewish religion, as the Jews perceived it, was that they were the chosen people and the promises of God were for them. They saw themselves as holy; and saw the non-Jews (Gentiles) as unholy. They often ignored the many prophecies that were given in the Old Testament about the Gentiles being brought into the covenant with God. In addition, women did not talk to strangers. This woman was a non-Jew; therefore, a Gentile, and considered unclean. The disciples would have considered her like a dog, and she might have known their attitudes. The story is repeated in Matthew, so I quote from both passages.

Mark 7:24" Jesus left that place and went to the vicinity of Tyre. He entered a house and did not want anyone to know it; yet he could not keep his presence secret. 25 In fact, as soon as she heard about him, a woman whose little daughter was possessed by an impure spirit came and fell at his feet. 26 The woman was a Greek, born in Syria. She begged Jesus to drive the demon out of her daughter.

27 "First let the children eat all they want," he told her, "for it is not right to take the children's bread and toss it to the dogs." 28 "Lord," she replied, "even the dogs under the table eat the children's crumbs."

29 Then he told her, "For such a reply, you may go; the demon has left your daughter."

30 She went home and found her child lying on the bed, and the demon gone."

Matthew 15: 21 Leaving that place, Jesus withdrew to the region of Tyre and Sidon.22 A Canaanite woman from that vicinity came to him, crying out, "Lord, Son of David, have mercy on me! My daughter is demon-possessed and suffering terribly."23 Jesus did not answer a word. So, his disciples came to him and urged him, "Send her away, for she keeps crying out after us."

...28 Then Jesus said to her, "Woman, you have great faith! Your request is granted." And her daughter was healed at that moment.

This woman, whose name was not given, set out over the hills and cliffs to meet with Jesus. She had a need -- her daughter was tormented and suffering. Like any good mother, she wanted help for her daughter. She had heard of this water-walking miracle-working healing-the-blind Messiah, and she was going for it.

Jesus had left Israel and gone to Tyre; a city located in what today is Lebanon. He had left the Sea of Galilee where he had fed the 5000 and he went to Tyre, probably to get away from the crowds and to teach the disciples. It was here that He was disrupted by this woman, who was pleading for His help. His

83

response was somewhat surprising. There were three responses here: the disciples', her response and Jesus'. Which one is yours? If there is thanksgiving dinner today or tomorrow, who is welcome at your table, and why?

The disciples had been taught a lot of religion and it was still in them, just like new wine in an old wine skin. Just like when I got saved, a lot of values and attitudes came from the old me. The disciples had been taught that women and children were of less value than men, and they had been taught that Gentiles were unclean and sinners. This woman was in every way unqualified to approach a rabbi. She was a woman, she was Greek, that is she was a Gentile, not a Jew, and therefore a sinner. From the disciples' point of view, she should have left. Jesus paused to see their reaction. They asked Jesus to dismiss her. Why? Because she was unqualified.

What was her reaction? She could have been offended and left right then, thinking that she was not worthy, and they didn't want her. As a pastor, sometimes people complain that I was not there for them to help their child or fix their marriage. It is possible that I wasn't, but at the same time, they did not bring their child or their spouse for counselling; or if they did, the child or the spouse had no desire to be counselled. When people do come for help, all I really can do is point them to Jesus and His Kingdom principles. This woman was different; she wasn't put off by the attitudes of the disciples. She wanted Jesus no matter what. Sometimes people come to church and someone looks at them the wrong way, or doesn't look at them at all, and they never come back. Not her. Jesus was watching her, and He was impressed with her tenacity.

When she asked Jesus to heal her daughter, she must have believed that by His merc word He could deliver her—impressive! This is what He said in Mark7:27 "First let the children eat all they want," he told her, "for it is not right to take the children's bread and toss it to the dogs."

This sounds very offensive. Is He calling her a dog? The Greek word is a pet dog or puppy, and that sounds better, but still…Jesus was looking to see her response, with (I believe) a smile on His face. She was not put off, she was not running away, she was not crying; she responded in accordance to what she believed about Him: Mark7:28 "Lord," she replied, "even the dogs under the table eat the children's crumbs."

She understood through the Holy Spirit that Jesus' mission was going to be all about reaching the Gentiles. The Son of David was the Messiah, not only to Israel, but to all the world. The disciples had grown up believing what the Pharisees believed, that the Messiah was coming for Israel only, and that He had come to deliver them from their enemies, the Romans. They believed that Gentiles were unclean, and women were lesser than men. We often divide people into groups, those who are part of us and those who are not! What if we get all that wrong, and the people that we think do not belong, do? Jesus confronts those beliefs.

Who are these people whom Jesus welcomes into His presence? Who does Jesus invite to the table? In Matthew 9, Jesus eats with the sinners and again we see the Pharisees objecting: Matthew 9:11 When the Pharisees saw this, they asked his disciples, "Why does your teacher eat with tax collectors and sinners?" 12 On hearing this, Jesus said, "It is not the healthy who need a doctor, but the sick. 13 But go and learn what this means: 'I desire mercy, not sacrifice.' For I have not come to call the righteous, but sinners."

Jesus is preparing the disciples to have a heart for what the world calls sinners and what Jesus also calls lost. In other words, "get ready, disciples; you are to invite woman, children, men, slaves and free, gentiles and Jews to your tables. You might as well get used to it." The righteous ones are those who believe that they are 'good', and God owes a blessed life, while sinners are the ones who know they need mercy.

In Luke 14, Jesus gives this parable: 16 Jesus replied: "A certain man was preparing a great banquet and invited many guests. 17 At the time of the banquet he sent his servant to tell those who had been invited, 'Come, for everything is now ready.'

18 "But they alike began to make excuses. The first said, 'I have just bought a field, and I must go and see it. Please excuse me.' 19 "Another said, 'I have just bought five yokes of oxen, and I'm on my way to try them out. Please excuse me.' 20 "Still another said, 'I just got married, so I can't come.' 21 "The servant came back and reported this to his master. Then the owner of the house became angry and ordered his servant, 'Go out quickly into the streets and alleys of the town and bring in the poor, the crippled, the blind and the lame.' 22 "'Sir,' the servant said, 'what you ordered has been done, but there is still room.' 23 "Then the master told his servant, 'Go out to the roads and country lanes and compel them to come in, so that my house will be full."

I just came home from Liberia on a mission trip where I spent time with John Kpewoan, whose story I previously shared. John had started an orphanage in Monrovia, and around his table were 70 orphans, who looked to John and his wife, Cecilia, as mom and dad. Who qualified to sit around John's table? Homeless children without parents! The orphanage was built in 1999, four or five years after the civil war ended, where one tribe had fought another, thereby leaving many children without family. But John created a safe place for children of every tribe to live and be educated.

The Syrian woman understood that Jesus had not just come for the Jews. The bread was not only going to those within Jewish borders, but to all who are hungry. This was a shock to the religious establishment, including the disciples. What Jesus was saying was that His time had not yet come, but because of her faith His mercy was extended, even though it was not according to His timetable.

He honoured her by saying: Mark 7:29 … "Woman, you have great faith! Your request is granted." And her daughter was healed at that moment. The Son of David (another name for Jesus) had healed her daughter, even though she was a woman, a Gentile, and considered a sinner. He responded to her faith and humility and granted her the desires of her heart. She had touched His heart of mercy, even when He said what a Pharisee would have said, "...that it was wrong to take the children's bread and toss it to the dogs." (Mark 7:27)

So how do we approach Jesus? We come with our needs. We all have needs. We come humbly before Him as people who are not qualified. We come in faith. We come with a persistent heart. We call on Him not because of what we have done but because of what He has done for us. We come because He is full of grace and truth. And when we come, Jesus qualifies us to sit at the banquet table of Heaven.

I read a story of Genelle MacMillan as told by Jim Cymbala in his book Breakthrough Prayers. Genelle had come from Trinidad where she had left two children with her ex-boyfriend and was now living in New York with a new boyfriend, Roger. On Sept 11, 2001 she went to work at 8 in the morning. She worked at the North Trade tower on the 64th level. She was talking to some of her co-workers when suddenly they heard a big bang. They were told that a plane had hit the tower. She thought it was a little plane. Smoke was starting to come in under the doors, so they began to tape off the doors. Finally, after an hour someone declared, "We have to go. We have phoned and no one is coming." All fourteen of them descended the stairs. At the 13th floor, Genelle's shoe hurt so much that she had to take it off. As she bent down there was a big boom, and everything went black. As she became conscious, she realized she was lying underneath a stairwell and her hair wedged underneath some cement pieces pinned down her head, with the possibility of dying. Her parents had been Catholics, but as a teenager she had rejected God and had found no time for Him. She now enjoyed a wild lifestyle in New York. But facing death, she called upon God's mercy. She knew she didn't deserve it. She was unworthy and unqualified. She began to pray and felt the pain lessened when she prayed. She made a deal with God that if He would get her out of this mess, she would serve Him. The next day she heard a 'beep beep', and then a voice. She called out. They finally heard her but they couldn`t see her, so she found a hole where she stuck her arm through. Some man named Paul said, "Ì will hold your hand until you are rescued."

Twenty or thirty minutes later, she was brought out on a stretcher and her hand left his. She was the last survivor to be rescued after being buried for 27 hours. She was one of the only two who survived of the fourteen from her office. When she got to the hospital, she was told that she might never walk. He brother-in-law had come to read the Bible to her at noon hours. Her faith began to grow, and she felt that she would walk again. After a while she began to walk with braces, and they told her that she might have to live with them forever. Again, she felt convinced that Jesus had a different plan. By February 2002, she took off the braces and has walked without them since. When Roger showed up at the hospital, she told him that they had to separate until they got married. She had made a deal with God, and she was eager to fulfill her commitment to live for Him. In November 2002, they got married and today they serve Jesus together.

Genelle had a need to be rescued, and she knew she didn't deserve God`s mercy. In humility and in desperation, she called upon Him, believing that He could hear her. She fulfilled her side of the deal by beginning to live a life honouring God. She attended Bible study and went to church.

When she was hospitalized, she wanted to thank Paul. When she asked her rescuers about him, they told her that no one had held her hand. Since that time, she has shared her story on CNN and Guidepost, but no one has come forth and claimed to be the Paul who held her hand. God's mercy shows up when we least deserve it. His table is filled with people of faith reaching out for His mercy. Jesus tears down the dividing walls of Jew and Gentile, slave and free, male and female.

Why did it at first seem like Jesus was playing into the typical Jewish attitude towards Gentile women?

Why is this Canaanite woman so significant?

We often see people as 'us and them'.   We put people in boxes, justifying our differences and criticism of them.   Jesus breaks the dividing wall between Jews and Gentiles.   Do you place certain people groups in certain boxes, justifying your animosity towards them?

Who qualifies to sit at your table?

Pray: Help me, Jesus, not to see people as those who are for or against what I believe, but as people who are all created in the image of God and in need of His love.   Help me, Jesus, to tear down dividing walls between people.

11. Who Do You Say I am?

Read the Gospel of Mark Chapter 8

"Who do people say I am?" Jesus asked the disciples in Mark 8:27. 28 They replied, "Some say John the Baptist; others say Elijah; and still others, one of the prophets."

When I asked my sister in Denmark who Jesus is, she answered, "A myth". Her answer was less glorifying than calling Jesus John the Baptist or a prophet; nevertheless, the most important question is, "Who do you say I am?" How that question is answered determines whether we live in error or in truth. The question of identity is everything. Peter answered by saying, "You are the Messiah."(Mark 8:29) That is, He is the anointed one. The word Messiah is the same word as Christ, it means the anointed one. The anointed one is repeated over 500 times in the Old Testament and 39 times in the New Testament. I was listening to Rev. Robert Morris, who explained that in the Old Testament, Israel was instructed to anoint three groups of people, the priest, the prophet and the King. Jesus is called the Messiah since He is anointed to be all three. According to Robert Morris, Jesus is saying, "I am your Priest, I am your Prophet and I am your King." A priest in the Old Testament entered the Holy of Holies on our behalf. He talked to God for you. However, through Jesus you can always talk to Him directly. Hebrews 4:16 Let us then approach God's throne of grace with confidence, so that we may receive mercy and find grace to help us in our time of need." A prophet heard from God and brought the message to Israel. When you are in Jesus, you don't need a prophet; you can hear from God yourself: "My sheep hear My voice."(John 10:27). The Prophet, Priest and King are all represented in one, Jesus.

The Jews expected a Messiah who would come as a conquering King. The Messiah would come to bring justice, end evil and make everything right. The Messiah would bring peace by overcoming the evil of Rome. The coming King would lead Israel out of oppression into victory. The Jews expected this kind of King. That is whom they thought of when they looked to Jesus and called Him the Messiah.

Therefore, the next thing Jesus teaches is a complete surprise to them — that He must be killed. It is not that He is going to be, but He must be. For the first time in the Gospel of Mark, the Messiah is now a suffering Messiah. The suffering Messiah and the coming King are one and the same person. Since Peter was a little boy, he was taught that the coming King was a conquering King not a suffering King.

We see where they get this hope from, as they would have read one of the many prophecies regarding the coming Saviour in Isaiah 9:6:"And he will be called Wonderful Counsellor, Mighty God, Everlasting Father, Prince of Peace.7 Of the greatness of his government and peace there will be no end. He will reign on David's throne and over his kingdom,"

They did not see the connection with Isaiah 53:5"But he was pierced for our transgressions, he was crushed for our iniquities; the punishment that brought us peace was on him, and by his wounds we are healed."

Jesus as a King was in many ways different than Old Testament kings and kings as we think of them. Kings rule and reign and so does Jesus. Beyond that there is little similarity. A king rules over a geographical area with real borders, Jesus reigns over a spiritual kingdom without geographical borders. Nonetheless, do not think that His kingdom is not as real as, or more real than, any physical kingdom.

Kings tend to live in castles or mansions completely sheltered from the common people, and they tend to live a sheltered and protected life. Jesus, on the other hand, steps out of His palace and begins his life on earth among the common people. He eats with the sinners and talks to them. I grew up in Denmark, which is one of the oldest kingdoms of the world. The queen's name is Margarete. Even though I am from Denmark, I cannot see her, eat with her or even have an official meeting with her. I don't qualify to be a guest and there is way too much security for me to even get close. With Jesus it is different.

Jesus stepped out of His heavenly castle and was born into a common family. Jesus ate with the sinners. Unlike kings protected by walls and guards, Jesus walked among people in the open where He frequently confronted His enemies. Kings live in comfort and safety. When there was a need to fight and lay down lives for a cause, the king would send out his subjects to the front line. Jesus, on the other hand, went to the front and laid down His life for His subjects.

When Jesus declared that He must die, Peter was quick to rebuke Him because it did not fit what Peter believed about the Messiah, as was the case with all the Jews. Jesus answered by saying in Mark 8:33 "Get behind me Satan." Sometimes we have the wrong concept of Jesus. Sometimes we think that He is like a Santa Claus who gives good gifts, or like a vending machine that spits out the right thing if we say or declare the right thing. However, Jesus came to deal with the evil of the world, or as it says in 1 John 3:8, He appeared "to destroy the devil's work" How? By healing the sick, forgiving people from their guilt and bringing them from a relationship with the darkness into a relationship with the Light of the world, Jesus Himself. In other words, by dying on the cross and extending a new agreement to all of us, Jesus did destroy the work of the one who has come to kill, steal and destroy. Evil might stem from the devil, but the reason that the devil has power is because our hearts are easily corrupted. Therefore, Jesus begins with dealing with our corrupted hearts. To stop evil, the heart must be transformed.

The way Jesus transforms the heart is to first deal with our debts. It is like in a courtroom. The devil can accuse us if there is any unforgiven guilt. We confess our sin and guilt to Him, and Jesus washes our sins away and declares to the devil "it is paid for." A transformed heart is an honest and humble heart that is willing to be transformed.

Fortunately, that is just the beginning of transformation; Jesus also deposits the Holy Spirit in us, giving us a desire to know God. As I tell my Bible study group who meets at 7:00 am every

Thursday morning, "You are here this early because the Holy Spirit has drawn you."

When I repented and asked Jesus in my life, the Holy Spirit gave me a desire to read His Word, attend Bible Study and church. The way your body craves water, the Holy Spirit craves the Word, and that is what transforms you.

Who does Peter say Jesus is?

What is unique about Jesus as King compared to an earthly king?

How does transformation take place?

Pray Dear Jesus; show me where the enemy might have a foothold of deception in my heart. Jesus, will You heal any area of my heart that is under the influence of the enemy.

12. Mountaintop Experience

Read the Gospel of Mark Chapter 9

The disciples saw Jesus perform miracles, saw Him forgive sin as if He were God, and declare Himself Lord of the Sabbath as if He wrote it. Peter has declared to Him: "You are the Messiah," (Mark 8:29) that is, the anointed One who has come to destroy the work of the devil. Nevertheless, for the first time, Jesus teaches that He must be killed, and this changes everything. This suffering and rejected Messiah was different from the One they expected. Jesus was to deliver evil, not out of the political system, but out of people's hearts, because ultimately that is what changes everything.

With this new view of the Messiah, it is time to affirm who Jesus is and the call of a disciple. It is time to prepare them for what they will encounter in the valley of life. It is time to prepare you for what is in the valley of your life.

Jesus brings Peter, John and James up on a high mountain. Most scholars believe that it is Mount Hermon (9000 feet). Jesus is bringing them into an encounter that will change their lives forever. Sometimes you must leave everything to seek His face. When they come to the top, the heavens open and they behold a view never seen before: Jesus was transfigured. His clothes were "dazzling white, whiter than anyone in the world could bleach them."(Mark 9:3) They saw a glimpse of the heavenly Jesus, who for a moment steps into His true heavenly clothes, like superman revealing his identity when for a moment he puts on his super clothes.

Not only did they see Jesus, they saw Elijah and Moses who were talking to Jesus. Both have been dead, one 500 years and the other 1400 years before Jesus' earthly arrival. Nevertheless, here they are fully alive talking to Jesus. Both had mountaintop experiences, one as the bringer of the Law, and the other as God's prophet.

Peter is so overwhelmed that he doesn't know what to say and as John Ortberg points out in Faith and Doubt, "When you don't know what to say, don't say anything." This doesn't occur to Peter; instead, Peter suggests that they set up three shelters (the Greek word is tabernacles). Like most of us, when we encounter His glory and majesty, we want to live there. His presence is captivating, glorious and inviting. Who would want to leave?

As David writes in a psalm of longing:"One thing I ask from the Lord, this only do I seek: that I may dwell in the house of the Lord all the days of my life, to gaze on the beauty of the Lord and to seek him in his temple. 5 For in the day of trouble he will keep me safe in his dwelling ;"(Psalm 27:4, 5)

Then a glory cloud came and settled all around them. The glory cloud means that God is there in person yet shielded from them. When Moses went up the mountain to receive the two tablets for the second time, he asked God "Now show me your glory." God told him, 20 But," he said, "you cannot see my face, for no one may see me and live." (Exodus 33:20.) So what did God do? He displayed His very nature: 5 Then the Lord came down in the cloud and stood there with him and proclaimed his name, the Lord. 6 And he passed in front of Moses, proclaiming, "The Lord, the Lord, the compassionate and gracious God, slow to anger, abounding in love and faithfulness, 7 maintaining love to thousands, and forgiving wickedness, rebellion and sin. Yet he does not leave the guilty unpunished; he punishes the children and their children for the sin of the parents to the third and fourth generation." (Exodus 34:5-7)

The three disciples heard the voice of God the Father, "This is my Son, whom I love. Listen to Him!" This suffering Messiah, the King of Kings, is who He says He is. God the Father has placed His hand of approval and identity on Jesus, saying to any sceptics, "This is my Son." Jesus is not just a universal logical principle that held the universe together. The Greeks believe Logos was such a principle. No, Jesus is a person! He is more than a prophet, a priest or a king, He is a Son, and He is divine.

The three disciples knew that if they saw God face to face, they would die, and so when they opened their eyes they did not expect to live, but there in front of them, they saw God's glory, Jesus. The very character of God is embodied in Jesus. Jesus is compassionate and gracious. And true, God will not let any guilty go unpunished, and for that very reason Jesus came. He came to pay the price for our guilt that we might go free from our past.

How do we receive His glory?

Many years later when Peter is trying to convince people about the authenticity of their witness, Peter refers back to this experience as he writes: 16 "For we did not follow cleverly devised stories when we told you about the coming of our Lord Jesus Christ in power, but we were eyewitnesses of his majesty. 17 He received honour and glory from God the Father when the voice came to him from the Majestic Glory, saying, "This is my Son, whom I love; with him I am well pleased." 18 We ourselves heard this voice that came from heaven when we were with him on the sacred mountain."(2 Peter 1)

Notice how Jesus received honour and glory when the Father's presence showed up and the Father declared, "This is my Son, whom I love."   When Jesus prays His last recorded prayer just before He is crucified, John writes:

20 "My prayer is not for them alone. I pray also for those who will believe in me through their message, 21 that all of them may be one, Father, just as you are in me and I am in you. May they also be in us so that the world may believe that you have sent me. 22 I have given them the glory that you gave me, that they may be one as we are one— 23 I in them and you in me—so that they may be brought to complete unity." (John 17)

That same glory that was given to Jesus on that mountain, according to Peter, is now also given to us.   How did Jesus give it to us? The same way He received it from His Father; by depositing His presence in us through the Holy Spirit and by declaring that we are His sons and daughters.   This is what Paul writes: 15 The Spirit you received does not make you slaves, so that you live in fear again; rather, the Spirit you received brought about your adoption to sonship. And by him we cry, "Abba Father." 16 The

Spirit himself testifies with our spirit that we are God's children." (Romans 8)

Jesus had two powerful mountaintop experiences. On the mountain of transfiguration, we see Jesus among two heroes of faith, Moses and Elijah, and we see Jesus in His resurrected and glorified form. But on Mount Calvary, Jesus seemingly lost all His glory and is now crucified among two thieves. On that cross, all human dignity was stripped off Him to the extent that He was unrecognizable. He was rejected, spat on and beaten to near death before He was nailed naked to a cross. Jesus took all our sin and shame so that we could receive His glory. He took our ashes that we might be clothed with His righteousness and crowned with His glory. What an exchange!

What does glory mean?

How do we receive the glory of Jesus?

What exchange took place at Mount Calvary?

Pray: Holy Spirit, make me aware of God in me. May I recognize the Lord's presence all around me. Teach me, Lord, how to embrace Your presence. May Your glory emanate from me.

13. How to go down that Mountain?

Read the Gospel of Mark Chapter 9

Peter wanted to stay in God's presence and in the fellowship of the saints. To Peter's and our disappointment, however, we cannot stay there, at least not until God calls us home. There is a life to be lived below the mountain. Peter and the other two disciples needed that experience to do what they were called to, and what they were called to, took place below. You also need a mountaintop experience discovering Jesus so you too can go down the mountain and face the world that you are not of, but that you are called to. Paul writes: 17 now if we are children, then we are heirs—heirs of God and co-heirs with Christ, if indeed we share in his sufferings in order that we may also share in his glory."(Romans 8) That sharing in His suffering is to be found below the mountain. It is time to go down your mountain. It is time to leave church and face Monday. They went down, and sure enough, the peace was broken, and the reality of the world challenged them.

The rest of the nine disciples were having a problem that caused an argument. The problem was with a man who had brought his son in need of being delivered from an evil spirit. They had done what they had seen Jesus do, but with no result. Rather than comforting the father and son, they ended up in an argument with a religious teacher. I don't know what that teacher would have objected to, but maybe he said something like this, "Who do you think you are, to pray in the name of Jesus, a false prophet?" The world wants to argue with you.

When Moses came down from the mountain the first time, after being absent for 40 days, he saw a golden calf built by the Israelites out of gold jewellery. Moses was angry because they had made a statue of a god of their own imagination. They wanted a god they could see.

In today's world, the atheists would claim that we have made Jesus in our own imagination. In our need for God, we created one. The problem with that argument is that many of us were not even looking for God when we miraculously discovered faith. Like Saul who became Paul, some of us openly resisted God and yet despite our rebellion, we discovered Jesus. When I look back on my salvation after surrendering and asking Him in my life, I see how God was working on my life long before that took place. He was placing me in a position where I could hear and see Jesus. I did not choose Jesus, I did not create Him out of my need for Him; He pursued me, and He chose me.

I read about the Chinese underground church telling their communist neighbours about God, using the human embryo as an example. As the child grew in the womb it probably thought initially that there was no life here and after. But as it grew arms and legs, it might have dawned on the child that they were to be used for something other than a life in the womb. In other words, there must be a birth.   In the same way, the hunger humans have for finding God and their willingness to spend their lives seeking Him, might very well point to an eternal reality of life after death with God.

The Sadducees say there is no resurrection, no afterlife and no demons or angels. In their view, there is no spirit world.   The Pharisees disagreed with the Sadducees on all those points.   Unlike the Sadducees, they believed in an afterlife and a spiritual world. Both groups would agree that there is no salvation outside the law, and that Jesus could not possibly be the Messiah.

When the disciples had an argument over deliverance, it was probably with the Sadducees who did not believe in the spiritual world.   The North American world is probably closer to Sadducees, they believe there is a god, but with no direct influence on their lives and no room for the spiritual realm. What will win the argument; however, are not words but a demonstration of God's power.   What greater demonstration than your love for them and your testimony?

After the mountaintop experience, the arguments seemed so shallow.   The three disciples have just seen Jesus glorified and the dead made alive.   Jesus is more than a priest, prophet and king, He is divine. What was their problem?   The problem was faith.   'You unbelieving generation', Jesus calls them.   He is not merely talking to the disciples but to all the Jews.   He is talking to us. When He comes back, is He going to find faith on this earth?   The disciples had enough faith to try but missed the anointing that comes from fasting and prayer.

The father was desperate, as any good parent would be to see their son healed.   'I have gone to every healer, every significant person coming to town. I prayed every prayer I could think of and made offerings to see him healed but to no help. When I heard of you, I came but you were not here, so I asked the disciples and they tried and failed. 'He said these doubting words: "if you can do anything, take pity on us and help us. (Mark 9:22) "If you can" are doubting words, words from the valley. But who can blame him after trying so hard and in addition, seeing the disciples' failed attempt? Then Jesus gives us the key to miracles, 23 "'if you can'?" said Jesus. "Everything is possible for one who believes." (Mark 9:23)

What do you do when it fails? Ask Jesus.

When you come down the mountain you will encounter failures, and then it is paramount that you know what to do. Most churches give up on the supernatural because they failed. They prayed and nothing happened. What then?

Moses encountered God on a mountain in a burning bush. When he went down the mountain, he encountered Pharaoh. Pharaoh is symbolic of Satan, who keeps people in bondage. Moses said, 'Let my people go,' the answer was, "No, I will not. Who do you think you are, demanding me the most powerful man of the world to free my slaves?" (my paraphrase) Here is what the Bible said:

Exodus 5:5 Afterward Moses and Aaron went to Pharaoh and said, "This is what the Lord, the God of Israel, says: 'Let my people go, so that they may hold a festival to me in the wilderness.'"

2 Pharaoh said, "Who is the Lord, that I should obey him and let Israel go? I do not know the Lord and I will not let Israel go."

Why should he, this was a cheap work force, no dental plan, unemployment insurance, pensions, or wages and only a little

104

food? Pharaoh ordered that the slaves were to make bricks without straw. The problem was, now the Hebrews were furious at Moses. His enemies were stacking up against him. He was alone with Aaron. What thought might have gone through him, "What a failure you are, how stupid can you be to have trusted God?"

Moses cried out to God and God answered with a promise.

Exodus 5:22 Moses returned to the Lord and said, "Why, Lord, why have you brought trouble on this people? Is this why you sent me? 23 Ever since I went to Pharaoh to speak in your name, he has brought trouble on this people, and you have not rescued your people at all."

When the nine disciples at the bottom of the mountain were approached by this desperate father who was looking for Jesus, much to the father's disappointment they would have answered, "He is not here." "Well," the father may have responded, "Could you help me?" They would have tried as they recalled what Jesus had done, but when nothing happened, they stood embarrassed and confused just like Moses. However, they did what all of us need to do in a similar situation, they asked Jesus: Why couldn't we? Jesus told them that it required prayer and fasting. The prayer is needed, I believe, to build their faith, and to give the Holy Spirit permission to lead. When nothing happens, ask Jesus why not and then lean upon His promise.

Exodus 6:6 Then the Lord said to Moses, "Now you will see what I will do to Pharaoh: Because of my mighty hand he will let them go; because of my mighty hand he will drive them out of his country."2 God also said to Moses, "I am the Lord."

Faith comes from a promise. Romans 10:17 "Consequently, faith comes from hearing the message, and the message is heard through the word about Christ." When you are in the valley, you need to find a promise. I was going through a very difficult time; people were leaving the church and the finances were going down. I asked the Lord for a promise, and this is what He gave me verse 20 "I answered them by saying, "The God of heaven will give us success. We his servants will start rebuilding, but as for you, you have no share in Jerusalem or any claim or historic right to it." (Nehemiah 2 and 2 Chronicles 20:15.)

I was listening to a testimony by Chris Gore. He is currently a pastor in charge of healing at Bethel Church in Redding, CA. Chris had a dream where he entered heaven. He was talking to Abraham when Abraham said, "Look behind you." Chris turned around and saw a gate and on the other side of the gate, there were thousands of people. Chris asked, "Who are those people?" Abraham answered and said, "They are people who have never experienced my love. Now go back and touch them with the love of God. Don't hammer them with the Bible but show them the Love of God." When he came back 'to earth' he went to a bank where there was a teller who was sick. He told her, "Jesus loves you." She replied, "No, He does not." Chris repeated it and the Holy Spirit fell on the teller causing her to drop to the ground weeping. The other tellers looked to see what was happening. Chris told them the same thing and they all fell under the power of the Holy Spirit, experiencing His love.

Even though he had prayed for over a thousand people to be healed to this point with no result, within the next few months, Chris saw thousands of people being healed. He travels to India and many places in the world where he sees the blind eyes open and deaf hear. He sees all kinds of diseases healed. But then he shares his failures of unanswered prayers. He tells the audience how a girl with a spinal disease, causing her not to walk and causing nightly seizures, has been prayed for over fourteen years every day and no breakthrough. "This girl," he says, "is my daughter." What do you do when your own daughter is not healed? Do you give up? At the bottom of the mountain of no healing for your own family, you must decide what to do. Chris had heard God say to him: "When someone is not healed, that is not your burden and when someone is healed, it is not your glory." Chris believes that God can do the impossible and that He loves his daughter. He also believes that there is a mystery that he might not have answers to on this side of heaven.

Coming down from the mountaintop experience is when the real test of faith is. Have you had one of those down the mountain experiences, when somehow it did not turn out the way you thought?

Interestingly, the disciples asked Jesus what was wrong, and He gave them an answer. What was the answer?

We may not always have answers to why or why not some prayers are answered. Are you okay with that?

Pray: Dear Jesus, help me in the valleys to do what You called me to do, and that is to help people be free. Help me to know how to fast and pray that others might be free.

14. Spiritual Pride

Read the Gospel of Mark Chapter 9

Mark 9: 33 They came to Capernaum. When he was in the house, he asked them, "What were you arguing about on the road?" 34 But they kept quiet because on the way they had argued about who was the greatest. 35 Sitting down, Jesus called the Twelve and said, "Anyone who wants to be first must be the very last, and the servant of all."

The disciples had seen Jesus preach with authority, deliver a boy possessed by a demon, heal the blind and deaf, and make a cripple walk. They saw Him walk on water, calm the storm and feed 5000 people with five loaves and two fish. They saw Him as the Messiah, the Lord of the Sabbath and as Divine. No one had ever seen what these twelve disciples had seen.

So, it was not surprising that they were arguing about who should be the greatest. Spiritual pride is as destructive as any other puffed up ego. The witch in the Walt Disney movie called Snow White looked in the mirror and asked," Who is the most beautiful of all?" When the mirror did not answer as she had expected, she got mad. Jesus addressed the tendency in all of us to be proud, crying, "Look at me, myself and I, us three!"

When I go to pastors' conferences, often a pastor will inevitably ask me how my church is doing and then he will wait to see if I will ask him the same. If I ask him the same, he will then with glee in his eyes, proceed to answer by sharing how many hundreds were in his church last Sunday. Something then rises in me. I want to compete, "Well we had 31 at kid zone." At the end of that conversation, I feel jagged. Pride and boasting brings out the worst. That is why Apostle Paul writes in 2 Cor. 11:30 "If I must boast, I will boast of the things that show my weakness." It is what I cannot do; only He can do that which brings glory to His name.

No one wants to be insignificant; we all want to be noticed. My grandson frequently would say "Watch me, Grandpa." While he would take my hand and show me a picture he had made or how he could stand on his head. But if our motivation for doing things is to get people's applause, we cannot follow Jesus, because sooner or later we will have to either please the crowd or Jesus.

This is what Jesus says about people who want to be seen, Matthew 6:2 "So when you give to the needy, do not announce it with trumpets, as the hypocrites do in the synagogues and on the streets, to be honoured by others. Truly I tell you, they have received their reward in full. 3 but when you give to the needy, do not let your left hand know what your right hand is doing, 4 so that your giving may be in secret. Then your Father, who sees what is done in secret, will reward you."

When we are proud, we want to blow our own trumpet, and usually it is at the expense of others. Frequently, I will come on a snowy Sunday morning and see the snow removed from the sidewalk and the steps in front of the church. It's the same fellow doing it and he is in desperate need of affirmation, but if that is the only reason he is doing it, then that is all the reward he will get. We need to thank people and honour them for their work, but in the Kingdom, it cannot be the key motivation for why we are doing it. This is what Paul writes in Col 3:17 "And whatever you do, whether in word or deed, do it all in the name of the Lord Jesus, giving thanks to God the Father through him."

President Trump may be considered the most powerful man today, but around 700 years before Christ, there was his equal with the name of Nebuchadnezzar, who ruled most of the eastern world. He saw himself as a god and demanded that people worship him. This is what you find in Daniel 4:4 "I, Nebuchadnezzar, was at home in my palace, contented and prosperous. 5 I had a dream that made me afraid." In other words, this king needed nothing. Like my niece said, "Why do I need God, I have everything." However, this king had a disturbing dream of a tree that reached into heaven. The wild animals lived under the shade of the tree and the branches were full of birds. Then a messenger came from heaven and cut down the tree. Daniel, the Hebrew slave turned prophet, interpreted the dream as the tree being Nebuchadnezzar. Even though he saw himself as god, the reality was that he was a vulnerable human and God was about to humble him. He was about to lose his mind and live among the animals. Twelve months later we see the dream come true.

Daniel 4: 28 "All this happened to King Nebuchadnezzar. 29 Twelve months later, as the king was walking on the roof of the royal palace of Babylon,30 he said, "Is not this the great Babylon I have built as the royal residence, by my mighty power and for the glory of my majesty?" 31 Even as the words were on his lips, a voice came from heaven, "This is what is decreed for you, King Nebuchadnezzar: Your royal authority has been taken from you."

See how proud he is of what he has done. There was no recognition of others or God, he did it all by himself. It was all about him. Then he lost his mind and his glory, and began to live like an animal. Some have said that losing your mind is being delusional, which is indeed what pride is. You think you are something you are not.

1 Cor. 4:6 "Then you will not be puffed up in being a follower of one of us over against the other. 7 For who makes you different from anyone else? What do you have that you did not receive? And if you did receive it, why do you boast as though you did not?"

You fail to see that what you have you did not earn, but you received it. Your life, your brain, your abilities to work and to make wealth, your salvation and your eternal life do not come from you, all good things come from God. Finally, after nine months, when Nebuchadnezzar regained his mind, he also gained the right focus as He gave thanks to the true Giver of gifts.

Daniel 4:37"Now I, Nebuchadnezzar, praise and exalt and glorify the King of heaven, because everything he does is right, and all his ways are just. And those who walk in pride he can humble."

Can you get your eyes off others and yourself, and onto Jesus, and begin to give thanks for all that He has given you, and out of that begin to serve Him? What enables you to serve with the right motive is knowing His amazing love that has been lavished on you. This is what Paul writes in 2 Cor. 5:14 "For Christ's love compels us, because we are convinced that one died for all, and therefore all died.15 And he died for all, that those who live should no longer live for themselves but for him who died for them and was raised again."

I was reading a testimony of Tass Saadat, "Once an Arafat Man." He was an Islamic Palestinian who became a sniper in Yasser Arafat's army. His father tricked him to get him out of the PLO so he could get an education and not be an Israeli and Lebanese target. To remove Tass from danger, he sends him to the US for him to go to college. Tass ended up working in a restaurant, washing dishes. He quickly learned to cook and became the manager of the restaurant. Eventually, he ran a restaurant business for a chain of hotels. Initially Tass had become married for the selfish reason of getting a green card and had every intention of divorcing his wife; however, after a year his wife was pregnant, and he had become very fond of his stepson from a previous relationship. So Tass stayed in the marriage, although he was not faithful to her. Finally, during a financial crisis, he lost his job. He went back to where he had started his career with the hope of buying that restaurant.

One day Tass confided in one of his regular customers named Charles that he was living with fear. Charles pointed upwards and said, "That is because you are not connected." All night this bothered him and offended him. Tass was a Muslim and therefore, believed that he was as much connected to god as anyone. A few days later he went and visited Charles to ask him about being connected. Charles opened the Bible and began to read John 1, "In the beginning was the word, the word was with God and the word was God."Tass began to shake and in a vision saw a light and heard a voice, "I am the way, the truth and the life." Tass felt the love of

God flood his soul and with Charles, he bent his knees and asked Jesus to forgive him. Tass had hated the Jews all his life and now he bent his knee to one.   Today Tass has a ministry to the Palestinians, and also to Jews.   Like Nebuchadnezzar, Tass was humbled and given a powerful opportunity to change.

Why is pride such a block to experiencing Jesus?

There is a promise in 1 Peter 5:6 "Humble yourselves, therefore, under God's mighty hand, that He may lift you up in due time." The journey up in the Kingdom is the way down to become a servant. Do you want to become Christ like? In what area do you resist being a servant, towards your family, coworkers or neighbours?

Pray: Dear Jesus, give me the same attitude that You have:

Phil 2:5 In your relationships with one another, have the same mindset as Christ Jesus:

6 Who, being in very nature God did not consider equality with God something to be used to his own advantage; 7 rather, he made himself nothing by taking the very nature of a servant being made in human likeness.

8 And being found in appearance as a man, he humbled himself by becoming obedient to death - even death on a cross!

15. What Am I still Missing?

Read the Gospel of Mark Chapter 10

Sometimes Jesus answers a question in a way that is not at all expected. A young man who was known as the rich young ruler (from the two accounts in Matthew 19 and Luke 18), fell on his knees and asked Jesus, "Good teacher," he asked, "what must I do to inherit eternal life?" The fact that He was referred to as a rich and young ruler meant that he was probably very religious and part of the Sanhedrin. Yet, he knew something was missing and, in his humility, he bowed before Jesus.

You would expect Jesus to say, "Repent for the Kingdom of God is near," or merely declare, as He did to Nicodemus, "You must be born again." Instead, Jesus enquired first why he called Him good: 18 "Why do you call me good?" Jesus answered. "No one is good—except God alone?" (Mark 10:18) I do not know why Jesus does not declare Himself to be God, but it is as if He is playing into how this young man sees Him as a special Rabbi with special powers, but not as God. People were drawn to Him, even though they did not know who He was. As a former atheist, I was drawn to the goodness of Jesus. I saw that He could heal the crippled, touch the lepers, raise a widow's dead son, and feed five thousand hungry people. Finally, now for my salvation, I saw Jesus hanging on the cross for my sins. The more I studied Jesus, the more I saw His goodness and I was drawn to Him. In contrast, the more I studied Mohammed, the more I was repulsed by him. He had thirteen wives; he even married a nine-year-old. His religion grew through violence. Jesus was very much the opposite of any religious person I had ever met. In the same way, this young ruler had never met anyone like Jesus, and that is why he called Him good.

In the eyes of a Pharisee, you inherited eternal life by being obedient to the law, so when Jesus answered him what he was lacking, Jesus answered in Mark 10 as a Rabbi would have: "19 You know the commandments: 'You shall not murder, you shall not commit adultery, you shall not steal, you shall not give false testimony, you shall not defraud, honour your father and mother.'"

In other words, be obedient; and as Jesus probably expected, the young man said, 20 "Teacher," he declared, "all these I have kept since I was a boy." I suppose that the young ruler had expected Him to say, "Well done, good and faithful servant, your place in Heaven is guaranteed." But He did not. The young man knew that there was something missing. As a former atheist, I knew that if life only existed as a product of evolution, then all I could declare at the grave of every life was 'meaningless, meaningless'. I knew that there must be more.

So, Jesus answered,21 Jesus looked at him and loved him. "One thing you lack," he said. "Go, sell everything you have and give to the poor, and you will have treasure in heaven. Then come, follow me."

There is no one else in the whole Bible to whom Jesus says, "Go, sell everything you have and give to the poor..." So why him? Jesus is not merely after a conversion or a sinner's prayer. He is after making disciples. He says, "...follow Me."Jesus knows that wealth is the one thing that will ensnare this man. He is saying to him, can you imagine what it will be like not to have servants, a fancy mansion, power to buy what you want or multiple means of transportation? The question is without all that will you still follow Jesus? He went away sad, for he had great wealth.

Why did God ask Abraham to sacrifice his son, Isaac? Abraham and Sarah had waited a long time for the promise of a child, and when all hope was gone, as Sarah was 90 and Abraham 100, God provided. When Isaac was around 13 or 15, God told Abraham to go and sacrifice him. Perhaps God knew that his child could become more important than his loyalty to God, so he needed to be tested. It is not that we are not to love our children; we are just not to love them more than God (see Matthew 11). Salvation is a gift of grace, but following Jesus costs us. That is why Jesus says in Mark 8:34 "Whoever wants to be my disciple must deny themselves and take up their cross and follow me. 35 For whoever wants to save their life[b] will lose it, but whoever loses their life for me and for the gospel will save it." Jesus will eventually point out the things that you need to confront, because they will trip you up if you do not. Hebrews 12:1-2 points out: "Let us throw off everything that hinders and the sin that so easily entangles. And let us run with perseverance the race marked out for us, 2 fixing our eyes on Jesus..."

When I was a new Christian, I hung onto my money. I had grown up in poverty. In our single-parent home, my mom brought home a small salary that needed to stretch. When I grew up, I had a poverty mentality, so I always lived in fear of not having enough. God began to deal with me by showing me that I needed to tithe and give to missions. Money would be a snare for me if I did not confront it head on. Jesus says in Matthew 6: 24 "No one can serve two masters. Either you will hate the one and love the other, or you will be devoted to the one and despise the other. You cannot serve both God and money."

Moses also had to deal with his own obstacle, fear. God knew that fear was what would ensnare Moses, so He set out to confront his fear. Moses meets God in a burning bush. God has heard the cry of the slaves and he is sending Moses. Moses' response in Exodus 3:11-12 is far from agreeable. "But Moses said to God, "Who am I that I should go to Pharaoh and bring the Israelites out of Egypt? And God said, "I will be with you." God promises this fearful shepherd and prophet that He will be with him. That, however, is not enough to calm Moses' fears. 13 "Moses said to God, "Suppose I go to the Israelites and say to them, 'The God of your fathers has sent me to you,' and they ask me, 'What is his name?' Then what shall I tell them?" 14 God said to Moses, "I am who I am. This is what you are to say to the Israelites: 'I am has sent me to you.' God had already told Moses who He was, God of Abraham, Isaac and Jacob, but now He adds:" I am who I am." God then demonstrates His power with two power encounters in Exodus 4:1, "Moses answered, "What if they do not believe me or listen to me and say, 'The Lord did not appear to you'?" 2 Then the Lord said to him, "What is that in your hand?" "A staff," he replied.

3 The Lord said, "Throw it on the ground." Moses threw it on the ground, and it became a snake, and he ran from it. 4 Then the Lord said to him, "Reach out your hand and take it by the tail." So, Moses reached out and took hold of the snake and it turned back into a staff in his hand. 5 "This," said the Lord, "is so that they may believe that the Lord, the God of their fathers—the God of Abraham, the God of Isaac and the God of Jacob—has appeared to you."

6 Then the Lord said, "Put your hand inside your cloak." So Moses put his hand into his cloak, and when he took it out, the skin was leprous—it had become as white as snow. 7 "Now put it back into your cloak," he said. So, Moses put his hand back into his cloak, and when he took it out, it was restored, like the rest of his flesh."

What is this lesson of the staff? Moses was called to more than a comfortable life in the back of the desert. Moses, like you and I, must learn to let go and let God turn his life into a miracle. Moses had to face fears and trust God.

Jesus deals with at least two different false ideas. The preconceived idea was that if you obey the Law then you will be blessed and if you are rich that means the blessing of the Lord is on you. The false idea is that every good person will inherit eternal life. The reality is that no one can be good enough. Jesus sets the bar of righteousness when He says that if you as much as lust for a woman then you have committed adultery (see Matthew 5:28). Jesus concludes with saying that with man it is impossible to be saved but with God all things are possible (Matthew 19:26).

Like the rich young ruler, Ali grew up in Pakistan and was among the elite. His stepfather was a lawyer and they lived in a fancy house with servants and cars. As a Muslim, he visited the mosque every Friday for prayer. As a teenager his future was secured, he would go to the best school and as part of the Higher-Class; he would get the best jobs. Everything went well until one summer when his mother sent him to England for the holidays to stay with his aunt. His aunt was in a wheelchair suffering from some disease. To his shock he discovered that she hosted something that they called a Bible study in her home. He also learned that his aunt had written a book, so he asked if he could read it. She said, "I don't think you want to." She knew the price he would have to pay if he read it and believed. But one day he found the book on his bed. Ali was angry at his aunt; she had betrayed her Muslim faith and had become a Christian. A spiritual battle took place, raising many questions. Ali finally went with his aunt to church and surrendered his life to Jesus. I am telling this story to show you how Ali had to let go of a wrong view of a harsh and unforgiving God. However, not only did he have to let go of his views but now he also had to experience rejection from his family and at times had to run for his life. Ali paid a high price to be a follower Jesus. Being a disciple leads you to an abundant life but the road of surrender can be painful, as it is a road of letting go the things that might ensnare you to a temporary life. The young ruler had to sell everything, not because wealth is a problem, but love of wealth is. You might have to turn off the internet and stop going to the bar. (My Life on a Terrorist Hit List by Ali Husnain)

The young ruler was asked to let go of his wealth, because Jesus knew that it would keep him from following Him. Ask Jesus what He might want you to let go of so that it will not ensnare you and hinder your relationship with Jesus. Look at your screen time, social media and other distractions, will Jesus say turn it off and follow Me? Look at your addictions, such as to sports or work.

The young ruler took pride in being good according to the law. We don't become saved by being good but by surrendering to His Lordship. Ask Jesus if there are religious practices that make you feel proud, like going to church, prayer and fasting? It is not your religious practice that makes you good, it is Jesus and His Grace that makes you good. Are you ready to lay down your life and everything you hang onto tightly and let God show you the way to an abundant life?

Pray: Lord, show me if I am hanging onto things that keep me from following You wholeheartedly? Do I have things that I look to for identity and significance, independently of You, Lord Jesus? You say that "those who live in accordance with the spirit have their minds set on what the spirit desires," (Romans 8:5) So help me live a life in accordance with the Spirit, that I might have life and peace.

16. Elevating Yourself!

Read the Gospel of Mark Chapter 10

Jesus was about to give them power and authority to bring the Kingdom to the ends of the earth. However, Jesus knew that unless you have a servant attitude, supernatural power and authority eventually will be self serving and thereby lead to destruction. It was like the book I read called The Test, where a young man stands to inherit a fortune from his rich grandfather. The problem was that the grandson was spoiled, lazy and selfish. Therefore, when the grandfather died, for the boy to inherit the money he had to pass ten tests. Every one of the tests was meant to build character. When he finally passed the test and received the money, he was ready to use it for the betterment of society and not on himself. Similarly, Jesus is teaching them repeatedly about a kingdom attitude of servant hood. This theme of servant hood and humility was already given in Mark chapter 9.

Mark 10:35 "Then James and John, the sons of Zebedee, came to him. "Teacher," they said, "we want you to do for us whatever we ask.""

This is not a very humble way of asking. They are asking God to do what they ask of Him. But Jesus is not offended. Listen to the dialogue.

36 "What do you want me to do for you?" he asked. 37 They replied, "Let one of us sit at your right and the other at your left in your glory." 38 "You don't know what you are asking," Jesus said. "Can you drink the cup I drink or be baptized with the baptism I am baptized with?"

39 "We can," they answered. Jesus said to them, "You will drink the cup I drink and be baptized with the baptism I am baptized with, 40 but to sit at my right or left is not for me to grant. These places belong to those for whom they have been prepared." 41 When the ten heard about this, they became indignant with James and John. 42 Jesus called them together and said, "You know that those who are regarded as rulers of the Gentiles lord it over them, and their high officials exercise authority over them. 43 Not so with you. Instead, whoever wants to become great among you must be your servant, 44 and whoever wants to be first must be slave of all. 45 For even the Son of Man did not come to be served, but to serve, and to give his life as a ransom for many."

Jesus is about ready to be crucified within the next couple of weeks, and here they ask to be seated next to Him in His glory. They don't realize that His greatest glory is displayed at the cross. They are thinking of Him as being seated at His throne and they are seated next to Him as ministers in a government, exercising a high level of influence. But Jesus is looking, not at the throne, but at the cross, and if they knew what they were asking they wouldn't be asking for a seat on both sides of Him. When He was crucified, two thieves were executed beside Him as prophesied. Jesus tells

James and John that at some time they will be martyrs. Jesus said to them, "You will drink the cup I drink and be baptized with the baptism I am baptized with" (Mark 10:39).

Then Jesus goes onto address an issue of pride that we all struggle with. We want to be great, at least in other people's eyes. Why do we lie? Why do we gossip? Why do we expand the truth? Why do we criticize? Because we want other people to see us as better than what we are. When you are late for a meeting what excuse do you use, "I was caught in traffic, I had an urgent phone call, or it was my wife." All this while you know that the real reason you are late is because you planned badly. These tendencies to self glorify lead to a very destructive temptation called self justification. Jentezen Franklin says, "Our greatest temptations come in the face of our greatest justification."

Why were the disciples indignant? Do you think it was because they abhorred the wrong attitude, or because they thought they deserved it as much as those other two? My grandchildren are very sensitive to justice. If one has the iPad for ten minutes, then the other must have the same. If one can come and visit their Nana, then the others must also have a date.

In Genesis 3, we see this temptation for being great played out: Gen. 3:1"He said to the woman, "Did God really say, 'You must not eat from any tree in the garden'?"2 The woman said to the serpent, "We may eat fruit from the trees in the garden, 3 but God did say, 'You must not eat fruit from the tree that is in the middle of the garden, and you must not touch it, or you will die.'"

4 "You will not certainly die," the serpent said to the woman. 5 "For God knows that when you eat from it your eyes will be opened, and you will be like God, knowing good and evil!"

How did Satan tempt them? By telling them they could be like God. They fell for it, and then came the greatest of all temptations: what to do when you are exposed. God asked them why they were hiding, and they told them that it was because they were naked. This is the following dialogue: 11 And he said, "Who told you that you were naked? Have you eaten from the tree that I commanded you not to eat from?" 12 The man said, "The woman you put here with me—she gave me some fruit from the tree, and I ate it." (Gen 3)

The great temptation is to justify your actions. Adam blamed Eve, and ultimately, he blamed God Himself by saying: "The woman you put here with me." (Gen 3:12) Had Adam taken responsibility for his actions, things would have looked very different. In this case, Adam did something wrong, and he tried to justify it by doing something even worse, blaming others. Do we not do the same in order to look better than we are?

The Holy Spirit leads Jesus out in the desert and there He encounters three temptations by the devil. The one temptation is the temptation of greatness: Luke 4:5"The devil led him up to a high place and showed him in an instant all the kingdoms of the world. 6 And he said to him, "I will give you all their authority and splendour; it has been given to me, and I can give it to anyone I want to. 7 If you worship me, it will all be yours." 8 Jesus answered, "It is written: 'Worship the Lord your God and serve him only.'"

This is a similar temptation to what Adam and Eve experienced, but Jesus did not fall into the trap. However, His greatest temptation was to come later. In the desert He did not sweat blood as He did in the garden. In the garden, Jesus was waiting for the moment of His capture, and when the soldiers came; His greatest temptation was facing Him.

Matthew 26:53 "Do you think I cannot call on my Father, and he will at once put at my disposal more than twelve legions of angels?" Jesus was innocent. He had done nothing wrong. He was a victim of jealousy and envy. They were about to beat Him, pull His beard, flog Him with leather whips whose ends were tied with bones and then finally finish Him off by placing Him on a cross naked and humiliated. Jesus could have stopped it with one command. Thousands of angels could have protected Him and stopped the injustice. But Jesus refused to defend Himself because that was not the will of God. This is how it was described in Phil 2:8 "And being found in appearance as a man, he humbled himself by becoming obedient to death— even death on a cross! 9 Therefore God exalted him to the highest place and gave him the name that is above every name, 10 that at the name of Jesus every knee should bow,"

Because Jesus did not justify Himself, He was exalted. This is also your greatest test, to humble yourself rather than retaliate. 6 "Humble yourselves, therefore, under God's mighty hand, that he may lift you up in due time."(1 Peter 5)

The two disciples were asking Jesus to become great in the Kingdom. They wanted a ministry of great influence and they wanted the highest honour of being seated beside Jesus in His kingdom. They didn't know what they were asking. Sitting next to Jesus meant giving up their right to defend themselves and their right to exalt themselves, and it meant forgiving those who persecute them. Becoming great in the Kingdom of God means to serve the needs of others as Jesus did when He met the greatest need of all, the need for forgiveness of sin.

The one man in all the Old Testament who could justify carrying out revenge would be Joseph. His brothers sold Joseph as a slave for thirty silver coins. He was falsely accused by Potiphar's wife and subsequently sent to jail. Pharaoh had dreams no one could interpret except Joseph. The dreams prophesied that there would be seven years of plenty and seven years of drought. Pharaoh saw the hand of God upon Joseph and so he became Pharaoh's right-hand man. The drama comes to a climax when his brothers show up looking to buy some grain because of devastating drought in Canaan. They don't recognize Joseph, but he recognizes them.

Gen 45:4 Then Joseph said to his brothers, "Come close to me." When they had done so, he said, "I am your brother Joseph, the one you sold into Egypt! 5 And now, do not be distressed and do not be angry with yourselves for selling me here, because it was to save lives that God sent me ahead of you. 6 For two years now there has been famine in the land, and for the next five years there will be no plowing and reaping. 7 But God sent me ahead of you to preserve for you a remnant on earth and to save your lives by a great deliverance."

Can you see it? Joseph is standing in front of the very people who betrayed him, hated him and hurt him, but now he has the power and the law behind him to inflict revenge. Had he killed them, Pharaoh and all of Egypt would probably have cheered him on, declaring that he had every right to do that. When we eat of the forbidden tree, we implement what we consider justice. However, had he done just that, he would have missed God's plan and the very reason that he was exalted. What about us? Do we give into the temptation to retaliate?

What about King David? As I heard Jentezen Franklin say, "You might think that the greatest temptation was David being tempted by Bathsheba. That might have been his greatest weakness, but his greatest temptation was when he had the opportunity to kill Saul." David had killed Saul's enemy Goliath; he had won many of his battles and he was destined to marry Saul's daughter when everything goes wrong. The people sang that Saul killed thousands, but David killed ten thousand. Saul, overwhelmed with jealousy empowered by an evil spirit, threw a spear at him. Has anyone thrown spears at you -- that is, hurtful, critical and degrading words hurled at you as if they were pointed spears?

Saul chased David with thousands of men. One day, Saul stopped his pursuit to go into the cave to relieve himself, not knowing that David and his men were hiding in the shadows of the cave. David's men quickly encouraged him to use the opportunity to kill Saul: 1 Samuel 24: 3" He came to the sheep pens along the way; a cave was there, and Saul went in to relieve himself. David and his men were far back in the cave. 4 The men said, "This is the day the Lord spoke of when he said to you, 'I will give your enemy into your hands for you to deal with as you wish.'" Then David crept up unnoticed and cut off a corner of Saul's robe.

5 Afterward, David was conscience-stricken for having cut off a corner of his robe. 6 He said to his men, "The Lord forbid that I should do such a thing to my master, the Lord's anointed, or lay my hand on him; for he is the anointed of the Lord." 7 With these words David sharply rebuked his men and did not allow them to attack Saul. And Saul left the cave and went his way."

127

David's greatest temptation came when the chance to kill Saul was given to him as a test. Would he obey his desire for revenge, and give in to the pressures of his generals, or would he obey God? All of Israel might well have applauded as they welcomed their new king. David passed the test; obeying God was more important than for David to fulfill his own sense of justice. Let God be our avenger.

The disciples would become great as they saw their persecutors, not as enemies, but as people Jesus loved. This is what Paul writes in Romans 12 when the Christians were persecuted by a Roman regime very hostile to Christians:

19" Do not take revenge, my dear friends, but leave room for God's wrath, for it is written: "It is mine to avenge; I will repay," says the Lord. 20 On the contrary:

"If your enemy is hungry, feed him; if he is thirsty, give him something to drink.

In doing this, you will heap burning coals on his head." 21 Do not be overcome by evil, but overcome evil with good."

Ask Jesus what it means to become great in His eyes.

Why was it important that Jesus didn't defend Himself at the cross?

Why is it important that we also don't justify our actions?

All of us have a sense of justice and want revenge when someone hurts us. Ask the Holy Spirit why is it so important that we turn the other cheek and forgive?

Pray, Lord help me to understand what it means to lay down my need to exalt and justify myself. Are there people whom I still need to forgive, and let God be the avenger?

17. The Cost!!! "Is He Worth it?"

Read the Gospel of Mark Chapter 10

What does it cost to be a disciple? In Mark 10:28, the disciples tell Jesus that they have given up everything to follow Him, but for what? Is He worth it? Jesus tells two parables about the Kingdom: Matthew 13:45 "Again, the kingdom of heaven is like a merchant looking for fine pearls. 46 When he found one of great value, he went away and sold everything he had and bought it."

44 "The kingdom of heaven is like treasure hidden in a field. When a man found it, he hid it again, and then in his joy went and sold all he had and bought that field."(Matthew 13)

While salvation is free and received by faith through grace in the power of the Holy Spirit, following Jesus costs you. When you are saved, Jesus asks you to follow Him as a citizen of the Kingdom of God, in obedience and in worship. This journey costs you something and maybe even everything. In the two parables, the treasure and the pearl represent your relationship to Jesus. If you listen to the people from the persecuted church, they would have had to face the cost and decide whether He is worth it.

Even though in this country our lives are not threatened with death because of our beliefs, there still is a price to pay, a price that you need to pay if you want the Heavenly Rewards. (see Luke 6:23)

Except for one, the disciples paid with their lives. Matthew died as a martyr in Ethiopia. Captured in Alexandria, Mark was dragged by horses through the streets until he died. Luke was executed by hanging in Greece. The rumour is that John faced torture by being dipped in a barrel of boiling oil, and supernaturally survived and subsequently was exiled to Patmos where he wrote the book of Revelation. Peter was crucified upside down in Turkey. James, the leader of the church in Jerusalem and Jesus' half brother, was thrown down from the temple and survived, but was then beaten to death. James, brother of John, was beheaded in Jerusalem. Nathaniel was a missionary in Asia when he was martyred by Armenian's whip. Andrew was crucified in Greece. Thomas was stabbed with a spear in India. Jude was killed with an arrow. Matthias was stoned and beheaded. Paul was tortured and beheaded. Are you ready to sign up?

In Mark 10:28: "Then Peter spoke up, "We have left everything to follow you!" 29 "Truly I tell you," Jesus replied, "no one who has left home or brothers or sisters or mother or father or children or fields for me and the gospel 30 will fail to receive a hundred times as much in this present age: homes, brothers, sisters, mothers, children and fields—along with persecutions—and in the age to come eternal life."

Jesus is saying that you will receive a larger family even if your own disown you. I can go to Kenya, Rwanda, Liberia, Denmark and around the world, and find brothers and sisters in Christ. In certain countries, people who turn to Jesus will lose their families, especially in the Islamic countries, but they will gain a spiritual family. I heard of a pastor in Russia who was imprisoned, and his wife and children were moved to Siberia. They were starving and feeling abandoned, "Does our father actually know where we are?" the children asked. The mother bravely answered, "No, but our Father in heaven does." That night in the freezing cold, God woke up an elder from a nearby church and told him to go and bring some food to this family. The elder complained that it was cold and that his horse might die and that he might never come home. God told him that He didn't ask him to come home, He just asked him to go. So, he went and gave them food and promised that more would come. The Father did know.

As I see it there are at least three different costs that a believer might experience:

1) Persecution. 2) Transforming love. 3) Spiritual battle.

In North America we are not experiencing persecution the way believers do in closed countries, yet there is a level of rejection and mocking that is increasing in our society. Children and teachers ridiculing their faith are silencing my grandchildren in their schools. We tried to bring an Alpha program to the High School, the principal agreed, the teachers agreed, but one parent complained to the superintendent, and it was shut down. This is the reward for persecution: 1 "Blessed are you when people insult you, persecute you and falsely say all kinds of evil against you because of me. 12 Rejoice and be glad, because great is your reward in heaven, for in the same way they persecuted the prophets who were before you." (Matthew 5)

The second cost is more of a challenge to us in our Western culture because it goes to the core of what we believe.

Transforming love is a call to a higher level of living. I found this quote by Timothy Keller in his book, Jesus the King: "All life-changing love is substitutionary sacrifice." Timothy is saying that all love that changes a life has a price. Raising healthy kids means you sacrifice your time, energy and rest for their sake. If you ever reach out to help the broken and the lost, it will cost you. This is how Jesus predicts His willingness to pay the price for our transforming life.

Mark 10:32 "They were on their way up to Jerusalem, with Jesus leading the way, and the disciples were astonished, while those who followed were afraid. Again, he took the twelve aside and told them what was going to happen to him. 33 "We are going up to Jerusalem," he said, "and the Son of Man will be delivered over to the chief priests and the teachers of the law. They will condemn him to death and will hand him over to the Gentiles, 34 who will mock him and spit on him, flog him and kill him. Three days later he will rise."... Jesus says, Mark 10: 45 For even the Son of Man did not come to be served, but to serve, and to give his life as a ransom for many."

The word 'ransom' refers to the sum of money you pay to set a slave free. While we were still sinners, Christ died for us. We were enslaved to our past sin and shame. Only one way could we be free, and that is if someone would take our place and absorb God's wrath. Not only did Jesus absorb our deserved punishment, but He also rose again and granted us His inheritance by giving us a brand-new identity as sons and daughters of God. The moment this truth sets in your heart, the guilt lifts and you become transformed. This gift of salvation is free, but it cost Jesus torture, rejection and humiliating death. He literally became sin so that we could have

His righteousness.   Nevertheless, the greatest cost was not the physical pain, but the emotional pain of being separated from His Father. Jesus cried out in a loud voice, "Why have you forsaken me?" (Mark 15:34)

Jesus asked of us to love with a divine love. In John 15, His command is: "Love each other as I have loved you."(John 15:12) Without love, you cannot be His disciple. "God is love. Whoever lives in love lives in God, and God in them." (1 John 4: 16.) Jesus washed the disciples' feet and then asked them to follow His example and do the same. Jesus told a parable of a master who had made a big feast. He told his servants to invite the guests. The guests were too busy with excuses, so he told them to go and invite the crippled and the blind. Another place He told the disciples not to invite the people who can invite you back; instead, invite those who cannot. What reward is there in loving people who can love you back? Jesus told about the rewards of those who visit prisoners and those who give water to the thirsty.

We pay this price when we forgive. The transforming love requires that we forgive those who hurt us. Forgiving someone is like saying, "Yes, it hurts, but I am willing to pay the price and let God be the judge."   Transforming love means that I extend forgiveness the same way Jesus did to me, as He paid the ultimate price at the cross.

The third cost is the cost of entering a spiritual war. We often look at spiritual warfare as only involving people who have opened themselves up to the occult or worshipped other gods.   But spiritual warfare is much more subtle than that, and very much among us.   Satan came to steal, kill and destroy, but how does he do it? By lying and deceiving; he is the father of lies.   He does it by accusing the brethren. I have friends who were married and are now separated. When I asked why, they each answered that their partner had a Jezebel spirit. They accused each other of having that spirit. They use Revelation 2:20-23 to justify not having anything to do with a person who they claim has that spirit. So, my friends say that is why they cannot reconcile until there is deliverance. I listened to two women in our church who each claimed that the other had a Jezebel spirit to justify why they should not forgive.

It seems when the enemy steps into a church or marriage, all the teaching about forgiving, loving your enemy and returning evil with good goes out the window. The teaching about gossip and judging others reaches deaf ears. If the people involved in the two examples would just step back and see how the enemy is laughing, they might not be so eager to accuse. We had some people leave the church and therefore, some people attacked me as the pastor, saying, "Maybe it is time for you to go?" They could not see that to 'save the church,' they were lining up with what the enemy was doing. Another had listened to a teaching of financial prosperity that pointed out that the sowing should be planted in prosperous soil, and since we were struggling financially, they removed their tithes to another ministry that was more prosperous. This person did not see that all they were doing was playing into Satan's plan. The cost that we are to pay in this warfare is very much to turn the other cheek, to let love cover a multitude of sins, and to forgive.

We are called to bless those who hate us, and that is a cost in the war against Satan. God calls us to come in the opposite spirit. Hatred is to be returned with love, greed with generosity, bitterness with forgiveness, criticism with honour, and fear with peace and love. Transforming love restores relationships by choosing to love instead of seeking justice.

In The Insanity of God by Nick Ripken, Nick had ventured out in the world to interview people with testimonies from the underground church. He set out to answer the question, "Is He worth it?" The first stop was Russia, where he interviewed hundreds, but one stands out, the story of Dmitri. Dmitri had been in prison for His faith for 17 years under communist Russia. Dmitri and his wife's family had been Christian before the revolution. When Lenin and his army destroyed the churches and imprisoned the Christians, the church was forced underground. For Dmitri it started when he and his wife had three boys. One day he said to his wife, "You will probably think that I am insane...I know that I have no religious training whatsoever, but I am concerned that our sons are growing up without learning about Jesus. This may sound like a crazy idea...but what would you think if just one night a week we gathered the boys together so I could read them a Bible story and try to give them a little training they are missing because we longer have a real church?" (pg. 152) What he did not know was that his wife had already been praying about that. So, on every Wednesday night they opened the Bible and began to teach and sing songs. The neighbour from the village heard their singing and asked to join them.

Before they knew it 25 people showed up. The officials noted the gathering and came to Dmitri and told him he could not have church. He told them that he did not have church; he did not have a building and was not a trained pastor. They insisted that he stop. The next week 50 people showed up. Now the authorities acted, and both he and his wife lost their jobs and their children were thrown out of school.   By the time their house church was 75 in attendance; the officials showed up and beat Dmitri in front of the congregation.   An elderly grandmother stood and pointed her finger at the official and said, "You have laid your hand on a man of God and you will not survive." The next day the official had a heart attack. The week after, there were 150 people, and now Dmitri was thrown in jail.

Thousands of miles from home, he was placed in a cell no bigger than a small bathroom. According to Nick, he had two disciplines that kept him spiritually alive.   Every day he would turn east and begin to sing. The prisoners would predictably react in mockery as they banged their cups against the bars trying to drown him out. Dmitri was the only Christian. The second discipline he stuck to was taking whatever scrap of paper he could find and write down as many Scriptures as he could remember. He would place the Scripture on his pillow where the guards would find it.   He subsequently was beaten for it.

The guards tried to break him, and one day they succeeded. They told him that his wife had died and that his three boys were taken by the state to be re-educated.   Overwhelmed with despair, Dmitri called the guards and told them to bring the papers for him to sign the next morning. He would renounce his faith so that he could be released and go and find his sons. But in the night, he had a dream where he saw his wife and three boys praying for him. The guards had lied about his family. His wife had woken up in the middle of the night and called her three sons together. She did not know what was wrong, but she knew that Dmitri was in trouble. As they prayed, God allowed Dmitri to see them sitting together interceding for him. The next morning when the guards came with the papers, Dmitri refused to sign and refused to renounce his faith.

One day he found a blank piece of paper and a pen. He wrote Scripture on both sides, knowing it would cause problems for him. When the guards found it on the pillow, they took him and dragged him down the hallway to be executed. As they did, all fifteen hundred prisoners stood up and faced east and began to sing the songs they had heard him sing the last 17 years. The guards dropped him and asked, "Who are you?" A few weeks later he was released.

Are you willing to pay the price of being ridiculed by people for your faith?

Ask the Lord to help you show love, even to those who hate you and have betrayed you.

Ask Jesus to fill your mouth with praise in the midst of your crisis, and not to quit when the enemy wants you to run?

Pray: Thank You, Jesus, for loving me and granting me a brand-new life in You. Help me to be courageous and stand for You even when I am being mocked.

Teach me, Lord, to love the difficult people in my life. Show me the ones I need to forgive. Finally, give me tenacity and strength to come against the enemy when he wants to discourage me and make me quit.

18. My House Shall be called a House of Prayer for All Nations.

Read the Gospel of Mark Chapter 11

Mark 11: 15 On reaching Jerusalem, Jesus entered the temple courts and began driving out those who were buying and selling there. He overturned the tables of the money changers and the benches of those selling doves, 16 and would not allow anyone to carry merchandise through the temple courts. 17 And as he taught them, he said, "Is it not written: 'My house will be called a house of prayer for all nations?' But you have made it 'a den of robbers.'" 18 The chief priests and the teachers of the law heard this and began looking for a way to kill him, for they feared him, because the whole crowd was amazed at his teaching."

When you enter the temple, there is an uncovered outer courtyard surrounded by a wall. In this area, Gentiles and Jews mingled together from all over the known regions. As you walked around the outer courtyard, you would find an altar where the sheep or doves were being sacrificed. From the historian Josephus' claim, there could be up to 250,000 sheep being slaughtered on a

Passover day. To be able to offer up a sacrifice, however, you needed to buy an animal using certain temple coins. So, as a worshipper, you had to first exchange your coins. The astute businessmen used high exchange rates and when you bought the animals, they charged you inflated amounts. Consequently, the outer court had turned into a marketplace. Jesus was furious. So, for the second time, He turned over the tables and chased out the moneychangers. The first time was at the beginning of His ministry in the Gospel of John and this is at the end of His ministry; for in the coming week Jesus is crucified. This is one of His last statements and judgment of the current place of worship.

This is not the meek and gentle Jesus that we often see depicted, this is a furious Jesus who has zeal for His Father's house. The Temple was intended for people to encounter God's presence, to reflect on His goodness and to worship, but what Jesus saw was the greediness of people ready to take advantage of others. He called the church a den of robbers. This is a good reminder for us pastors that we should remember church is not merely about hosting people, but our church services need to cultivate the presence of Jesus.

Jesus declared the purpose of the church when He said, "Is it not written: 'My house will be called a house of prayer for all nations?' (Mark 11:17) The church is not just a house of preaching and a house of music, but also a house of prayer. The church is a place of communicating with our heavenly Father, to connect with Jesus our Saviour, and be filled with the presence of the Holy Spirit. Our worship is not just singing songs, but they are songs of prayer where we lift our hearts to Him in adoration and in intercession.

As pointed out by Tim Keller, Jesus is not merely declaring what is wrong with the temple being a marketplace, but He is announcing a completely different way of worship. The Jews saw the temple as the center of their religion. Every serious Jewish believer would make a pilgrimage to the temple at least once a year for one of the big celebrations. The temple was designed from the template that God gave to Moses for how to build the tabernacle in the desert. There was an outer court with an altar for sacrifice, then there was a big bowl, a Laver, that was meant for the priests to cleanse themselves. From there you walked through a curtain into the Holy Place accessible only by the priests. There on the left was a candle holder, the menorah, with seven candles. On the right was a table with showbread. Then in the middle was a place of burning incense. In front of you would be another curtain thirty feet tall, keeping us sinners from the Holy of Holies. In the Holy of Holies was the mercy seat, which covered the ark containing Aaron's rod, the tablets of the covenant and the pot of manna, and on top were two cherubim facing each other as if guarding the ark.

The only person allowed in the Holy of Holies was the high priest. He would go into the Holy of Holies once a year with a bowl of blood from a lamb. He would sprinkle the blood on the mercy seat for the sins of Israel. It was believed that if the High Priest in any way defiled the Holy of Holies he would die, so they tied a rope around him, and in that way, they could drag him out without themselves getting exposed to God's radiant and deadly glory. This was really a place of worship set up for the nation of Israel even though Gentiles were welcome in the outer court. The Jews believed that when the Messiah came, he would chase out all the foreigners.

Jesus declared that the church or temple was to be for all nations; that is, for every Jew and Gentile. As written in Ephesians, we are no longer aliens or foreigners but citizens of His kingdom. (see Eph 2:1) Rather than chasing out the Gentiles from the Temple, Jesus was saying that His Father's house is also for them. A few days later when Jesus hung on the cross and with His last breath pronounced, "It is finished," the curtain to the Holy of Holies ripped in half, signifying that the Holy of Holies is available to everyone. Jesus opened a way for all sinners to come to the most Holy place by cleansing us from our sins. Not only can we come into His presence, but His very presence comes to dwell within us. Like the temple we have three parts: body, soul and spirit. We become a holy temple, and that is why sexual immorality is the same as desecrating the Holy of Holies.

18 Flee from sexual immorality. All other sins a person commits are outside the body, but whoever sins sexually, sins against their own body. 19 Do you not know that your bodies are temples of the Holy Spirit, who is in you, whom you have received from God? You are not your own; 20 you were bought at a price. Therefore, honour God with your bodies."(1 Cor. 6)

What has all this to do with prayer? Peter tells us in 1 Peter 2:9 But you are a chosen people, a royal priesthood, a holy nation, God's special possession, that you may declare the praises of him who called you out of darkness into his wonderful light. 10 Once you were not a people, but now you are the people of God; once you had not received mercy, but now you have received mercy."

Peter tells us that we are a chosen priesthood. A priest offers up sacrifices of thanks to God, which is a form of prayer, and he/she stands in the gap between the hurting and lost world. We are called in prayer to declare the praises of Him who has brought us out of the darkness into the light and we have been called to cry out in humility for salvation to come to the lost. The church is meant for people to meet with God and to help others to meet with God.

The Temple was considered the center of the Jewish religion, but Jesus shocked the Jews when He said it was a house of prayer for all nations. What about our modern-day church?

In what ways may we have turned the modern church into a marketplace?

In what way is the temple an illustration of our three-part body?

How can we protect the Holy of Holies of our body from being desecrated?

Pray: Dear Jesus, help me to pray for all nations. Show me Lord if there is any way that I defile my spirit with movies, pornography, gossip, or anything else. Create in me a clean heart and give me a steadfast spirit. (see Psalm 51)

19. Mountain Moving Faith

Read the Gospel of Mark Chapter 11

Doubt builds them and faith tears them down!

Mark 11: 22 "Have faith in God," Jesus answered. 23 "Truly I tell you, if anyone says to this mountain, 'Go, throw yourself into the sea,' and does not doubt in their heart but believes that what they say will happen, it will be done for them. 24 Therefore I tell you, whatever you ask for in prayer, believe that you have received it, and it will be yours. 25 And when you stand praying, if you hold anything against anyone, forgive them, so that your Father in heaven may forgive you your sins."

This is no small claim. To tell an immovable, impenetrable, indestructible rock to move into the sea, that is impossible except by faith. If you believe that whatever you ask for, you have received it before you have it, it is yours. It is time to move mountains. What is this mountain?

I asked some Healing Lodge women what they considered immovable problems. They answered addiction, fear, depression, broken relationships and prison. Those are indeed mountains.

Nevertheless, what Jesus is saying is that the root of those mountains is unbelief. The question then is how do I find faith? Remember the man who came with his demon-possessed boy and asked Jesus if He can do anything? Jesus answered in Mark 9:23 "'If you can'?" said Jesus. "Everything is possible for one who believes." 24 Immediately the boy's father exclaimed, "I do believe; help me overcome my unbelief!"

There is nothing wrong with admitting that our faith is not where it needs to be, if the admission of unbelief turns us towards Jesus, the Author of our faith, who will answer us when we seek, ask and knock for more revelation. If you turn toward your unbelieving friends with your doubt, it will grieve God as much as a child rejecting a father's love. Trust His promise: He will reward those who earnestly seek Him. (Hebrews 11:6.)

Without faith it is impossible to please God. Faith is the substance of what we hope for and the assurance of what we do not yet see. Faith is a way of seeing the world through the eyes of God. Paul declares that we do not live by what is seen, but by what is unseen. What is seen is temporal, but what is unseen is eternal. When we look heavenward, the things of this world will grow strangely dim. When we fix our eyes on our mountains, the problems become bigger and more impossible, but when we look to Jesus, the Author of our faith, our trials become inconveniences.

1 John 5:4 "for everyone born of God overcomes the world. This is the victory that has overcome the world, even our faith. 5 Who is it that overcomes the world? Only the one who believes that Jesus is the Son of God."

Faith comes from hearing and hearing comes from the word of God (Romans 10:17). The truth is that to overcome your mountain

144

of issues, you need to receive a promise from God. Our pattern is usually: a problem, desperate prayer, God's promise, and God's provision. There is one thing missing in this sequence and that is purpose. God has a purpose for our lives and that is not just to make us comfortable and relieve us from pain, but to fulfil His dream, although He might use the pain to get us to our purpose. While we might only see our problem, God superimposes that into a bigger plan, His plan.

Sometimes, God sees a bigger mountain in front of our mountain, which needs to be dealt with before we can have faith to tell our mountain of problems to leave. He might see selfishness, pride and unforgiveness. The way to mountain-moving faith will always take us through a time of humility and repentance. To summarize, all sin is rooted in the sin of unbelief, and the mountain of unbelief is thrown into the sea by surrendering to God and His plan.

Jesus found Himself in the Garden of Gethsemane facing the biggest mountain that anyone could ever face. Naturally He prayed with great earnestness to see this mountain move. Mark 14:36 "Abba, Father," he said, "everything is possible for you. Take this cup from me. Yet not what I will, but what you will."

Jesus knew that the next day a whip made of leather straps with bones at the end would be used to rip his body to pieces. His beard would be plucked out and a crown of thorns would be placed on His head in mockery. He would be stripped naked and hung on a cross for the spectators to hurl insults and condemnation. He would be rejected, abandoned, forsaken and all the sin of mankind would be absorbed onto His body. No wonder He asked God to remove the cup of suffering. Sometimes God will not remove the mountain because it has a bigger purpose. Jesus' sacrifice would ultimately set billions free from their sin. The key to overcome, however, is Jesus' famous words, "Not my will but Your will be done." (Matthew 26:42)

I will say Jesus sees these three mountains: A) The mountains that you see that cause fear, worry and anxiety. B) Then He sees the mountains of character flaws. Mountains that we do not see very well, but nevertheless are problems that need to be overcome for us to get to our destiny. C) The last mountain is a mountain of purpose or destiny. When we enter the purpose that God has for us, we will encounter impossible obstacles that can only be overcome by the power of God.

Moses saw the injustice and cruelty against his own people as they were enslaved by the Egyptians for 400 years. He tried to fix it by killing one of the slave drivers. When he realized that he was found out, Moses fled into the desert until God got his attention by speaking to him out of a burning bush. (see Exodus 3). Here is the impossible mountain: over a million Jews were enslaved. They prayed, and God answered by sending Moses. Moses needed faith. He was not exactly welcome in Egypt since he was wanted for murder. So God gave him a promise: 12 And God said, "I will be with you." (Ex 3:12.) Jesus gave the disciples a similar promise when He said: "And surely I am with you always, to the very end of the age." (Matthew 28:20) Moses could not do it in his own strength, but now God says Moses can free the slaves because God will make it happen. The disciples, like Moses, are asked to do the impossible. They can only fulfill their call through the promise of God, that is; "I will be with you." This is not a small promise. The God of the universe will be with you. Then came the provision:

Moses leads the Jews by following a cloud by day and a light by night. God provides food and water supernaturally to over a million people.

What is your mountain? Have you prayed and asked for a promise? Let the Holy Spirit lead you.

Take the promise, pray it and declare it. I have frequently reminded God, "You promised me You would provide." Then I gave thanks for His provision before I saw any sign of it.

Have you seen the provision yet? Do not give up.

There was drought in Israel, but God had given Elijah a promise of rain. This is how he prayed: 43 "Go and look toward the sea," he told his servant. And he went up and looked.

"There is nothing there," he said. Seven times Elijah said, "Go back." 44 The seventh time the servant reported, "A cloud as small as a man's hand is rising from the sea." So Elijah said, "Go and tell Ahab, 'Hitch up your chariot and go down before the rain stops you.'" (1 Kings 18:43-44)

Pray: May I have as much faith as Elijah that I will not give up but declare God's promise until I can see the provision come through.

20. The Greatest Commandments!

Read the Gospel of Mark Chapter 12

A teacher of the law asked Jesus what the greatest commandment was. Mark 12:28 "One of the teachers of the law came and heard them debating. Noticing that Jesus had given them a good answer, he asked him, "Of all the commandments, which is the most important?"

29 "The most important one," answered Jesus, "is this: 'Hear, O Israel: The Lord our God, the Lord is one. 30 Love the Lord your God with all your heart and with all your soul and with all your mind and with all your strength.' 31 The second is this: 'Love your neighbour as yourself.' There is no commandment greater than these."

Jesus tells us what to focus on, or in other words, what to live by: loving God and others. If you ask people what principle they live by, or what overall advice they follow, you will often hear something like this: "Whatever makes me happy," or "whatever makes money". Summarize their answer and you have, "Love yourself with all your heart, soul and strength." If you listen to the grad speeches, the advice is to follow your dreams and the desires of your heart -- you can do all things. It all sounds good, but that is not the principle that God gives; in fact, God warns us against this way of life. These are the signs of the end times: 2 Tim 3:1 "But mark this: There will be terrible times in the last days. 2 People will be lovers of themselves, lovers of money, boastful, proud, abusive, disobedient to their parents, ungrateful, unholy, 3 without love, unforgiving, slanderous, without self-control, brutal, not lovers of the good, 4 treacherous, rash, conceited, lovers of pleasure rather than lovers of God—"

People who are lovers of themselves are miserable, self-centered, greedy individuals like Ebenezer Scrooge. He was obsessed with accumulating wealth. He used relationships to get what he wanted, took advantage of his employees, and begrudged having to give them Christmas day off. His heart was cold and indifferent to the needs of others until he had a visitation of the Christmas Spirit, (symbolic of the Holy Spirit) on Christmas Eve. This Christmas Spirit brought him face to face with his past sins of swindling and conniving. Finally, he realized that if he died that night, no one would grieve or miss him, but some might even rejoice. He pleaded for mercy. He woke up on Christmas Day realizing that God had granted him another chance. Scrooge became filled with generosity and love for others. A remarkable transformation had taken place! We call it being born again. This was a picture of the work of God's grace and mercy, and God's ability to open a man's eyes to see people as He sees them, with compassion and love.

When I first heard of Jesus, it was through some friends who invited us to a Bible study. My wife wanted to be able to answer our 5-year-old son's many questions about God. As an atheist, I went along because the people were nice, and the food was good, and I could tell them how dumb they were. They began to tell me about this Jesus who fed the hungry, who identified with the poor, who healed the crippled, who ate with the sinners, who took the little children and blessed them as He declared that the Kingdom belongs to such as these. That was a time when children were considered unimportant, not to be heard or seen. Similarly, women were not counted equal with men, but rather next to slaves and dogs, yet Jesus elevated them; for example, He chose a woman to become the first evangelist, who was the Samaritan women at the well. In the same way, He gave an example of honouring women when He invited Mary and Martha to be His students at a time when rabbis only taught men. Jesus was counter-cultural when the first people He revealed Himself to at His resurrection were women. Through these stories, and His ultimate sacrifice at the cross, I saw His heart of love. It was this heart of love that caused Jesus to take my place at the cross.

Jesus was stripped naked, torn to pieces with a whip with leather thongs strapped with bones. They called it being flogged when they were whipped until they were brought near death. Jesus had lost his strength and someone else carried His cross. Then with a crown of thorns they cursed his claim to be a king, they nailed Him to a cross and raised Him up among two thieves for the world to see. All His glory and honour were stripped off Him as He was reduced to a criminal in the eyes of the world while He was falsely accused. It was a sacrifice offered for me and you. I deserved what Jesus voluntarily received. You may laugh and say, "No one deserves that!" I did. Jesus is holy, God is holy, The Holy Spirit is holy, but I am not. My heart, my mind and my will have lived in mockery and in rebellion against God. If you take all your thoughts and put them on the wall as a running screen, you will soon see how your thoughts are far from godly. Jesus absorbed all my sins and the sins of the world, past, present and future. So why should I not love Him with all that I have? Who else would ever do for me what He did? "While we were still sinners, Christ died for us." (Romans 5:8)

Jesus tells us: 12 My command is this: Love each other as I have loved you. (John 15: 12) That is easier said if that is your child or beloved relative, but what if that is your enemy? This is what Jesus says in Matthew 5:43 "You have heard that it was said, 'Love your neighbour and hate your enemy.' 44 But I tell you, love your enemies and pray for those who persecute you, 45 that you may be children of your Father in heaven. He causes his sun to rise on the evil and the good and sends rain on the righteous and the unrighteous. 46 If you love those who love you, what reward will you get? Are not even the tax collectors doing that? 47 And if you greet only your own people, what are you doing more than others? Do not even pagans do that? 48 Be perfect, therefore, as your heavenly Father is perfect."

We might love to justify our anger and resentment towards another person, but Jesus does not give us that option. The question is how can we love others with His love, when our neighbour does not return that love? I talked to a friend of mine who had been treated terribly by her mother. She told me that she cursed her mother every day even though her mother was dead. I need to tell you who have been abused and mistreated that this message of love does not mean that justice does not need to take place or that abusers do not need to be stopped. It does mean that I will leave the justice to authorities and to Jesus. This message of love means that I will not take revenge in my heart towards my enemies. It is really a message that sets me free.

Corrie Ten Boom wrote a book called The Hiding Place. During the Second World War, her family owned a watchmaker store in Haarlem, Netherlands. When the Jews came for help, they hid them and helped them escape. One day one of their own fellow citizens spied on them and gave them up to the SS who imprisoned them. Her own dad died in the jail; her sister died in the concentration camp where Corrie was also imprisoned, and Corrie was accidentally released before the war was over. The rest of the women died in the camp. The people who were most hated in Holland after the war were not the SS, as much as it was their citizens who collaborated with Nazis. Corrie went on to build a home to protect these collaborators. Corrie knew that the hatred was the work of the spiritual enemy, Satan, and to stop the cycle of violence she had to come in the opposite spirit. The response was to love your enemy. Corrie had learned this from her sister Betsie, who was lying ill beside her in the concentration camp. Betsie saw how Corrie was becoming bitter, and so she told her to be thankful. Corrie asked what she could be thankful for. "For the fleas, Betsie answered. The fleas keep the guards away and therefore we can have Bible studies undisturbed."

Today in the media we see politicians, Hollywood stars and sports heroes being accused of sexually harassing or raping women. The world is shocked and outraged by their sin. But what are we to do as followers of Jesus? What did Corrie do to the very people who betrayed her? She even forgave the guard who beat her sister when she came face to face with him following the war. We want justice and justice is required. The victims need to know that they are being heard and that action is being taken. The perpetrators are products of a society that has worshipped love of self. Many of us have to some extent applauded this slide into self-centred living. Many would silently agree with, "Whatever feels good, go for it." So why should we be surprised in the Me Too movement? I would agree that it exposes the sin and the root of a culture that has less and less moral convictions.

However, loving God means that we now see these famous sinners as people just like Scrooge or the Nazi collaborators, as people who are desperately in need of an encounter with the Holy Spirit. Their families, their kids and grandkids will all experience their dad's or granddad's disgrace. Their family name will be dragged into the mud as being sexual perverts. Our response is not to say we forgive them and let us agree to forget about it. No, they need to feel the consequence of their sin, but they also need to know that God does redeem and restore. They need us to pray for them and show them the love of Jesus: His redeeming, restoring and transforming love. His mercy is greater than judgment and so ours should be as well.

Loving God helps us overcome ourselves. It changes our priorities, and it changes how we see people and how we see ourselves. How do you love Jesus? How do you wish you loved Jesus? Loving your neighbour might very much mean to love your enemies. Do you have people in your life who are difficult to love?

Are there disappointments deposited against God in your heart that prevent you from loving Him wholeheartedly? Tell Jesus about it. Pray: Dear Jesus, show me areas of my life where trust might have been broken. Will You, Jesus, show me the truth? I welcome You into every broken part of my heart.

21. Loving God

Read the Gospel of Mark Chapter 12

Mark 12:30 "Love the Lord your God with all your heart and with all your soul and with all your mind and with all your strength.'[f

Loving God with all your heart helps you focus your life on what God desires for you, and it gives you a heart for others. In addition, loving God affirms who you really are as God bestows a new identity on you. The question is how can we love God with all our hearts? God's love is a reckless love that empowers you to love the unlovable.

How can you ever do that? You can only give away what you have. You may have a million dollars, you might have fame and a mansion on the hill, but in 1 Corinthians 13: 1-3 the Bible says if you do not have love, you have nothing. If you have spiritual gifts or even do good things for the poor, but have no love, you have nothing. We are created in the image of God who is love; that means we are created to receive it and to give it away. Love is more than feeling; it is giving of yourself. Love connects. Love moves you closer to the other person. It attempts to build a bridge. Love sees the best, believes the best, draws out the best. Love empowers you to see beyond the worst. Love overcomes a multitude of sins.

I love my wife, but sometimes I try to do it from a distance. Sometimes I feel hurt or offended and I give her the cold shoulder, or I pout or give her the silent treatment. Sometimes I want to control her so that she gives me what I want, and I use anger, persuasive words or become loud. In any of those cases, I create distance; in fact, all sin creates distance and is an enemy of love. You may even say, "I don't care about what you say, you can't hurt me." That is an attempt at creating distance. Love looks for a way to be reconciled. Love takes responsibility for its own action and reaction. When I embrace my wife and ask her to forgive me for having hurt her, I am decreasing the distance, even if she does not respond now. Remember, love does not demand a response.

When it comes to loving God, there is a challenge. While Jesus came in the natural, we do not have Him here now in the natural realm. So how can we connect or draw near to Him who is unseen? We worship Him in spirit and truth; therefore, we also love God in Spirit and truth. Many people believe that God is up there, and we are down here, and loving God means striving to please Him and hope that one day when we die, we will have His approval. That, however, is not Christianity; that is religion. Jesus came and became one among us. He came to seek and save the lost. When He left this earth, He promised the disciples that He would not leave them orphans but would send the Holy Spirit in His place. God is not far away; He is in us. Christ in you is the hope of glory (Colossians 1:27). Jesus tells us that we might be looking all over for the Kingdom when it is within us. So loving God is loving Him from within.

Since God doesn't move or change, the only way to bridge the gap between Him and us, is for us to make a step towards Him. The only way for me to be reconciled with my wife is to for me make a step towards her in repentance and surrender. If she initiates the reconciliation, I still must receive it and make that step towards her. When it comes to God, He has already made that step towards me and so it is up to me to make a step of repentance and surrender towards Him. I need to embrace Him as a little child would. That is obvious for those who have a relationship with Jesus; however, for the new believer as well as those who have been a Christian for a long time, there is one thing that prevents them from this step and that is trusting that God is a good God.

Adam and Eve walked with God in the Garden enjoying a perfect relationship with each other. Their connection with God the Father had never seen a challenge until Satan showed up with a sneaky temptation. He asked them if it was true that they must not eat of any of the trees in the garden. They answered him by saying that they could eat of all the trees except one, the tree called Knowledge of Good and Evil. If they ate of that tree, they would surely die. Satan then proceeded to lie to them, "You will not surely die... you will be like God." Genesis 3:4-5 The forbidden fruit looked delicious, and Eve took a bite and handed it to Adam. Forbidden fruit always looks good, and the thought might come, "Who can it harm?" Then they saw themselves as naked and went and hid. God came in the garden calling for them, "Where are you?" Genesis 3:9 When God calls, it is not because He does not know where you are, but sometimes we do not know where we are in relationship to Him. They came out of hiding, and as an excuse they said they were hiding because they were naked. "Who told you that you were naked? Have you eaten from the tree that I commanded you not to eat from?" God asked. Genesis 3:11 Adam said, 'she made me do it' and Eve said, 'Satan made me do it' (My paraphrase).

Adam and Eve had the opportunity to become reconnected with God if they only had taken responsibility for their actions; but they did not, instead they blamed their shame and guilt on one another. You may be a victim or a perpetrator of sin, but until you take responsibility for your own heart attitude and actions, you cannot be reconnected with God. The rest of the Bible is a story of God trying to reconnect with mankind, culminating in Jesus' crucifixion.

The issue behind the fall of man is not merely their disobedience or lack of repentance. Nor is the issue merely the human tendency to want to be his or her own god, and thereby not willing to subject themselves to anyone else. Rather, the real issue is God's goodness. Adam and Eve listened to Satan's lies, which led to doubting God's goodness. The thinking might go something like this, 'Is it really true that God does not want the best for us, our happiness?' The biggest struggle for Christians is to believe that God is good and He is for them. He has their best interests at heart. Many Christians might very well have become cynical over time especially if they were taught that following Jesus meant a blessed and easy life. The question then is what do we do with our unanswered prayers? What do we do about the sense of injustice or suffering that we see around us, but God seems oblivious to?

I heard a report from a Syrian refugee camp full of Christians whose family members had been executed by ISIS. They said, "Don't feel sorry for us, massive numbers of Muslims are turning to Jesus because of the violence they have seen done in the name of their religion." They saw how God was not wasting the sacrifice but turning it out for good. Yes, there are questions we will not have full answers to on this side of heaven, and one of the reasons for that is that we don't see the big picture. However, here is a promise from His word: 28 And we know that in all things God works for the good of those who love him, who have been called according to his purpose. (Romans 8:28)

The answer to the cynical and the anxious person is: "fixing our eyes on Jesus, the pioneer and perfecter of faith. For the joy set before Him, He endured the cross, scorning its shame, and sat down at the right hand of the throne of God'. (Hebrews 11:2) Start with throwing off what entangles you. King David was honest when he cried out, "My God, my God, why have You forsaken me?" Psalm 22:1 Moses was honest when He answered God with, "Who am I that I should go...?" Exodus 3:11 Gideon was honest when he complained that God had forsaken them. Tell the Lord how you have felt disappointed. Then admit to the Lord that His ways are bigger than yours. His plan is beyond your comprehension. Abraham struggled with trusting God's promise that his descendants were going to be as many as the sand on the seashore. While in prison, Joseph had no idea how God's plan would unfold. Facing a mob of angry Hebrew slaves, who had been told to make bricks without straw, Moses had no idea what it would take for Pharaoh to release the Hebrew slaves. The disciples did not know how Jesus was going to transform the world through them who were uneducated, fearful and despised by the world. Martin Luther King Junior had no idea how his non-violent social revolution was going to turn out when he was beaten and imprisoned, and many of his own followers wanted to turn to violence. When I began pastoring a church, I complained to God that everything that was happening in town spiritually was happening in the other church down the street. This new church was the result of a split from our congregation and one other church. God told me to stop looking over the fence and start looking to where He had called me. Bring your complaints and fears to God; bring the very things that are causing your heart to lack trust.

When Jesus knew that the disciples were going to face the greatest trial of their lives, He said: "Do not let your hearts be troubled. You believe in God, believe also in Me." (John 14:1) "...I will come back and take you to be with Me..." (John 14:3) Jesus affirmed His love for them. He wanted them to be with Him. "I will not leave you as orphans, I will come to you."(John 14:8) Jesus knew that they would feel disconnected from Him for a short time.

When you feel disconnected you need to know that Jesus loves you, not just because He must but because He wants to, so do not lose heart. These words penned by Apostle John are words for you also. Loving God with all your heart starts with you knowing that Jesus is for you and you can trust that God is a good God.

The second strategy to overcome hardened hearts is to look at, meditate upon, and declare all that God has already done. Do it in prayer, reading the Bible and in worship, praising Him with a grateful heart. Maybe your spouse is not saved yet and maybe you are still sick? Maybe you lost a family member way before their time should have been up. Maybe you lost your job. Maybe you failed your exam. Maybe a tornado tore down your house. Maybe your boyfriend dumped you. Paul says that He has learned to be content in all circumstances (Phil 4:11). How can Paul say that? Wasn't he beaten, shipwrecked, jailed, stoned and abandoned? And didn't Paul lose his career, security and pay as a Pharisee? The answer is: yes, that is him. Paul declares, "More than that, I now regard all things as liabilities compared to the far greater value of knowing Christ Jesus my Lord, for whom I have suffered the loss of all things-indeed I regard them as dung!-that I may gain Christ."(Phil 3:8 NET) This "all things" refers to all that he had accomplished in the world such as being one of the most highly educated people at the time and honoured within the religious power structure. All that was lost, but Paul did not get bitter or hardened by his trials; he became more and more a lover of God. Even though Paul is in prison, he is single minded in pursuing Christ. (Phil 3:12) Look how he frequently breaks out in praise, "Now to Him who is able to do exceedingly abundantly above all we ask or think..." (Eph 3:20.) For Paul, loving God with all his being does not mean a life without trials or a life without a price to pay, but a life laid down and at times enduring suffering as Christ endured suffering.

Listen to the story in Luke 7:36-50 when Jesus was invited to have lunch at Simon the Pharisee's house. A woman who lived a sinful life, most likely a prostitute, discovered where Jesus was eating, and she boldly entered the house. You can feel how the air was sucked out of the room as the Pharisee and his guests watched in shock when she knelt at Jesus' feet and began to cry. Her tears came like floodwater and wetted His feet. She then proceeded to

160

wipe His feet with her long hair and kiss them. Can you hear their thoughts? What about yours: 'gross, yuck, kissing feet and wiping them with her hair?' Then she opened the jar of expensive perfume and poured it on his feet. The aroma would have filled the room. The only ones with expensive perfume would be rich prostitutes or women who had saved up for the day of marriage (there is a similar story in Mark 14 where it is pointed out that the perfume was expensive). Jesus was touched by her love and sacrifice. However, the Pharisees were disgusted and wondered quietly why Jesus was not rebuking her, especially if He was supposedly a prophet. Here is a revelation; God knows your thoughts, even those quiet nasty ones. What does Jesus do?

Luke 7:40 Jesus answered him, "Simon, I have something to tell you." "Tell me, teacher," he said.41 "Two people owed money to a certain moneylender. One owed him five hundred denarii, and the other fifty. 42 Neither of them had the money to pay him back, so he forgave the debts of both. Now which of them will love him more?" 43 Simon replied, "I suppose the one who had the bigger debt forgiven." "You have judged correctly," Jesus said.

44 Then he turned toward the woman and said to Simon, "Do you see this woman? I came into your house. You did not give me any water for my feet, but she wet my feet with her tears and wiped them with her hair. 45 You did not give me a kiss, but this woman, from the time I entered, has not stopped kissing my feet. 46 You did not put oil on my head, but she has poured perfume on my feet. 47 Therefore, I tell you, her many sins have been forgiven—as her great love has shown. But whoever has been forgiven little loves little."

48 Then Jesus said to her, "Your sins are forgiven." 49 The other guests began to say among themselves, "Who is this who even forgives sins?"

Why did this woman do what she did? Loving the Lord comes from a revelation of who He is and what He has done, and it leads to a sacrifice.

What just happened? Where did she get that love from? I have heard it said that those who do not love God do not know Him. (Mark Batterson, 'If', Page 23) She just lavished her love on Jesus because she knew Him in ways that others do not. She walked into someone else's house and fell on her face crying. I suspect that she might have heard of Jesus or seen Him in action healing people, hanging out with sinners, and even eating with them. She found Him safe. She risked rejection, scorn and humiliation, yet she did it anyway. Do you find Him safe? So safe you can raise your hands in worship no matter what people think? Do you find Him so safe that you can bring all your guilt to Him? The Bible says that Jesus is gentle and humble at heart. She knew the depth of her shame and guilt. She knew what people like Simon thought of her. By the power of the Holy Spirit, she had a revelation of the truth; Jesus held the key to her broken shame-filled heart. Her tears were tears of pain and relief. Here was someone who could lift off the weight of her past.

I have seen prisoners whose shame is written all over their faces. Their guilt is tormenting them because of how they have hurt their children through their addiction and crime. When I explain to them Jesus' mercy and forgiveness, a weight comes off them and you can literally see their countenance change. They frequently turn around and try to make amends with their families. Phone calls are made, and letters are written. I get comments like the one I received the other day: "Hans, I just spoke to my daughter for the first time in seven years. I asked her to forgive me. Now she wants to see me. I cannot believe it!" She loves much because her many sins have been forgiven.

One Healing Lodge resident asked me: "So we know we are sinners, but what about Simon or those who have not sinned. Does that mean that they cannot love God very much?"I wrote my name on the board and said, "You probably consider me someone without sin, but I tell you that all depends on how you measure it." If you use Jesus' measuring stick, I am as guilty as anyone. I have lied; I have stolen from my mother's cookie jars and lied about it. The Bible calls that being a thief. I have lusted and Jesus says that is as bad as committing adultery. I have hated people in my heart and that, Jesus says, is the same as committing murder. Simon did not love much because he did not see his own sin as clearly as he could see hers. Jesus tells us, "Do not judge or you too will be judged. For in the same way you judge others, you will be judged, and with the same measure you use, it will be measured to you."(Matthew 7:1-2)

We have all sinned, we have all fallen short. Like swimming across the channel from France to England, you might have swam halfway, while another swimmer made it three quarters of the way; in either case, you both needed help or you would have drowned. While our sin might differ in severity and consequences, we are all sinners. Truly this woman expressed genuine repentance, which is what leads to loving with the whole heart. On the one hand, repentance is a gift from God; on the other hand, it is a willingness to submit to the truth. She demonstrated her love because she knew something Simon did not. She knew that Jesus can set you free to become something that your past will not allow you to become, a new creation. If you truly know Him, you will love Him.

This woman demonstrated something else about loving God. She paid a price, not to earn His love, but to give herself wholeheartedly to Him. The cost she paid was twofold. She risked rejection and humiliation by coming there. If you want to love Jesus with passion, you must risk your reputation. You must overcome your own fear of people. The second cost is her alabaster jar of perfume. Some believe that this might have cost her a full year's wages. If you are not willing to let go of your possessions for Jesus, then do you really love Him? The Bible teaches us to be rich towards God and store up treasures in Heaven. (Luke 12:21) Worship is more than singing songs; it is lavishly giving to His Kingdom work. Loving God with your heart also means loving Him with all you have.

John Wesley wrote many books, and he was a wealthy man in comparison to others at the time. He made over 1400 pounds annually. John Wesley kept 30 pounds for himself per year and donated the rest. John believed that you should only keep for yourself what you needed to live on and give the rest towards spreading the gospel. He considered others who did not practice this generous lifestyle 'Dead Christians'. Authentic Faith by Gary Thomas, page 177. Does God need this money any more than He needed an alabaster jar of perfume? No, but where our heart is that is where our treasure is. We cannot love God and money at the same time. The way to overcome the love of money and the fear of lack is to give to the Kingdom even when sometimes it stretches us. Lavish giving is like perfume to Jesus.

Knowing Him will lead you to love Him. I just read a book by Nik Ripken called The Insanity of God. The book is full of stories gathered from interviews with the persecuted Christians from 74 nations. He tells the story of Aisha on page 294. She was the young wife of a radical Muslim, Mahmoud. Mahmoud stirred up trouble against a Christian-run clinic located across from his shop. One day, however, he was deadly sick with cancer and so people stopped coming to his shop thinking that the cancer was contagious. The Christians from the clinic reached out to him and before he died, he became a believer and so did Aisha. She became an effective evangelist. Finally, the police Chief had her arrested and thrown in a dark hole beneath the police station. The hole had no lights and was full of rats and insects. In fear, she wanted to scream, "God, I cannot do this anymore." Rather than a scream, however, words of a song came. She began to sing to the Lord. Upstairs in the station it became very quiet. After one day, the Chief of Police for the city opened the lid and brought her out. He took her to her home and told her that he wanted her to come to their house in three days and explain to him and his family why she was not afraid. The love of some Christians brought the love of God to the wife of a radical Muslim. In her love for Jesus, she could not keep her mouth shut. She came face to face with fear, but in overcoming that fear through a song, she witnessed to the most powerful man of the city. Knowing God leads to loving Him, and that translates into loving even those who persecute you.

'Loving' God means trusting that He is a good God. In what ways is Jesus a good God?

How did the woman in Luke 7 love Jesus? Why?

How can we love with the same passion?

165

Pray: Dear Jesus show me all that You have done for me again. Help me to love You with an abundant love. Give me a passion for You. May I love You for who You are not merely for what You can give me.

22. Loving your Neighbour.

Read the Gospel of Mark Chapter 12

What is the most important thing you can do on this side of heaven? You have on average about 85 years if you are a male, or 87 years if you are a female. What are you supposed to do with that? This is how Jesus answers that question:

A lawyer comes and asks, what is the most important commandment? Mark 12:29-31"The most important one," answered Jesus, "is this: 'Hear, O Israel: The Lord our God, the Lord is one. 30 Love the Lord your God with all your heart and with all your soul and with all your mind and with all your strength.' 31 The second is this: 'Love your neighbour as yourself.' There is no commandment greater than these." What is this love of your neighbour?

According to Martin Luther King, "Love is understanding, redemptive goodwill for all men, so that you love everybody, because God loves them. You refuse to do anything that will defeat an individual, because you have agape (love) in your soul. And here you come to the point that you love the individual who does the evil deed, while hating the deed that the person does. This is what Jesus means when he says, "Love your enemy." Martin King Junior (Delivered at Dexter Avenue Baptist Church, Montgomery, Alabama, on 17 November 1957.)

In my own opinion, love is when you want to see the other person becoming all that God has created them to become. Love is, therefore, not necessarily giving that which another demands or wants, but giving them what they need to become Christ like. As parents, we know that if you just give your child what they want, you might very well destroy them. If you give addicts what they want, you might very well destroy them. Sometimes your love might not be received or perceived as love now. God tells us that He disciplines those He loves. God might withhold His blessings for a season to get us where He needs us to be. This type of love allows you to separate the sinner from the sin, as Martin Luther pointed out.

Jesus says to the disciples in John 15: 34-35 "A new command I give you: Love one another. As I have loved you, so you must love one another. By this everyone will know that you are my disciples, if you love one another." This is no small task; you are to sacrifice as Jesus sacrificed. Love costs you something; if it does not, it is not love. Many people use people, control people, flatter people and manipulate others and they call it love. But it is not love. Love believes the best. Love sees the treasure planted by God in another human. Jesus called Simon: Peter -- which means rock -- long before Peter was a rock. Jesus calls us sons and daughters long before we behave as if we have a heavenly Father. Love means calling forth what God says about them. Love indeed covers a multitude of sins.

Our Lord, however, increases the bar for the expression of love. This is what He says in Matthew 5:43 "You have heard that it was said, 'Love your neighbour and hate your enemy.' 44 But I tell you, love your enemies and pray for those who persecute you, 45 that you may be children of your Father in heaven. He causes his sun to rise on the evil and the good and sends rain on the righteous and the unrighteous. 46 If you love those who love you, what reward will you get?"

What Jesus saying is that we are to love those who do not even like us, people who might want us harmed; we are to see them as God's creation and people whom God loves. Our hearts are to desire that they will become all that God has created them to be.

There was a different lawyer in Luke 10 who asked Jesus how he can inherit eternal life. Jesus asked him what the great commandment is, and he answered correctly quoting Deuteronomy, but as he quoted the second command, to love your neighbour as you love yourself, he "wanted to justify himself, so he asked Jesus, "And who is my neighbour?"(Luke 10: 27-29)

30 In reply Jesus said: "A man was going down from Jerusalem to Jericho, when he was attacked by robbers. They stripped him of his clothes, beat him and went away, leaving him half dead. 31 A priest happened to be going down the same road, and when he saw the man, he passed by on the other side. 32 So too, a Levite, when he came to the place and saw him, passed by on the other side. 33 But a Samaritan, as he traveled, came to where the man was; and when he saw him, he took pity on him. 34 He went to him and bandaged his wounds, pouring on oil and wine. Then he put the man on his own donkey, brought him to an inn and took care of him. 35 The next day he took out two denarii and gave them to the

innkeeper. 'Look after him,' he said, 'and when I return, I will reimburse you for any extra expense you may have.'

36 "Which of these three do you think was a neighbour to the man who fell into the hands of robbers?" 37 The expert in the law replied, "The one who had mercy on him." Jesus told him, "Go and do likewise."

To understand this story, we need to be reminded about how much animosity there was between the Jews and the Samaritans. Because of some history of the Samaritans attempting to prevent the rebuilding of the temple, and because they were considered half breeds, the Jews hated them. They were enemies. This lawyer is a man of the Law of the Old Testament, and he is a racist. The reason I say this is because of how Jesus tells the parable. When Jesus asks a question or tells a parable He often does it in such a way that it exposes the heart of the inquirer; for example, when they brought the woman caught in adultery, they told Jesus that according to Moses' law she should be stoned, but what did He say? They were all standing with their stones ready to stone her.

In the same way, Jesus tells this parable explaining not so much who his neighbour is, but how he becomes a neighbour. The people who passed by were busy doing their religious thing going to Bible studies and prayer meetings, or maybe they were busy with hockey or dance lessons. When it came to the Samaritan, however, he stopped to help this man who was a stranger and an enemy. He bandaged him, probably by ripping his own shirt into strips. He poured oil on the wounds and then he took this half-naked man and placed him on his donkey, took him to a nearby inn, told the innkeeper to take care of him no matter the cost. It was like giving the innkeeper a blank cheque to spend whatever he wanted. Then came Jesus' question, "Who is the neighbour?" The lawyer had to admit that it was the one who showed great mercy. The lawyer could not get himself to say the word Samaritan, so he said the one with great mercy.

What was Jesus calling us to? He is calling us to care for those in need, whatever their religion, nationality, social status or whether they are friend or enemy. A good neighbour is someone who loves, especially those who are difficult to love.

Martin Luther King spoke these words: "You have left the world cluttered with communities that surrendered into hatred and violence."

We are going to follow another way. We will not abandon our righteous efforts, we will continue to rid the nation of segregation and we will in the process not relinquish our privilege to love while abhorring the segregation. We will love the segregationist. This is the only way to build a loving community. To our bitter opponents we shall say, "We will meet your violence with soul-ish force. Do to us what you will, and we will continue to love you. Send your hooded perpetrator into our community and beat us and we will still love you. But be assured that we will wear you down with our love."

Loving your neighbour can be difficult especial if they hate you and look down on you as in the case with Martin Luther King Junior. Still Jesus calls us to return hatred with love. Do you have people in your life that you need to extend a hand of love? I do, a good friend left our church, and when I saw him a while back, he gave me the cold shoulder. I need to do my part and extend a hand of love.

In our community we can easily talk bad about immigrants or Muslims. However, Jesus loves them. Think again, are there groups of people that you have placed in a negative light? How can you be a neighbour to them?

Pray: Dear Jesus, forgive me for any people I have built a case against that has prevented me from loving them. Show me Lord how I can extend a hand of love to the people who hate me?

23. Be Alert, He is coming!!

Read the Gospel of Mark Chapter 13

Mark 13:32 "But about that day or hour no one knows, not even the angels in heaven, nor the Son, but only the Father. 33 Be on guard! Be alert! You do not know when that time will come. 34 It's like a man going away: He leaves his house and puts his servants in charge, each with their assigned task, and tells the one at the door to keep watch.

35 "Therefore keep watch because you do not know when the owner of the house will come back—whether in the evening, or at midnight, or when the rooster crows, or at dawn."

The disciples were walking through Jerusalem a few days before Jesus was crucified and they walked by the temple. They marvelled at the stones that weighed several tons. You can see some of the original stones today by the Wailing Wall and they are indeed impressive. Then Jesus shocked them when He prophesied that the stones would be torn down. They asked Him when this would happen. Jesus went on to warn them that there would be deception from false teachers. He warned of wars and rumours of wars.

Jesus told them to be on guard because of persecution. He also mentioned national catastrophes such as earthquakes and drought. While Jesus prophesied somewhat general events, He suddenly said something that was specific. The gospel would be preached to all nations. The last one is measurable, and many believe it can be done by 2025. The other specific prophecy is that the walls would come down, which they did in 70AD. Many believe that this might very well happen again. Prophecies often work that way; they refer to something immanent and something in the future.

The point behind Jesus' warning is that we need to be ready to meet Him. Whether we meet Jesus because we die, or we meet Him in the air because He returns, the warnings are the same, be ready to meet Him. Salvation is by grace, and nothing we can do will earn our salvation; however, after we are saved, we need to work out our salvation. What we do with what God gives us is eventually judged or rewarded. The life we live as believers does count.

1 Cor. 3: 12 If anyone builds on this foundation using gold, silver, costly stones, wood, hay or straw, 13 their work will be shown for what it is, because the Day will bring it to light. It will be revealed with fire, and the fire will test the quality of each person's work. 14 If what has been built survives, the builder will receive a reward. 15 If it is burned up, the builder will suffer loss but will be saved—even though only as one escaping through the flames."

The things we do for His glory will be rewarded; and the things we do for our own glory or for someone else's glory will be like the wood, straw and hay, and will be burned up. The things that we do for His glory will be like gold, silver and costly stones, and will withstand the fire and leave us with crowns purified through fire.

174

In Matthew 25, Jesus gives a parable to illustrate that what we do with our talents, money, time, and work is like three servants who are being given 5, 2 and 1 talent to invest. The master came back after a long while and asked what happened to his investment. The two servants had multiplied their talents to 10 and 4 talents. The master was very pleased and called them good and faithful servants. But the servant with one talent had buried the talent because he thought that the master was a hard master who reaped what he had not sown. This servant was punished with a pink slip on which was written, "fired".

The point is that Jesus holds us accountable for the gift and talents He has given us. We do not all have the same talents or abilities and so we cannot compare ourselves to others, but we all have been given something that is needed. Therefore, use what you have been given. Invest your talents and abilities into the Kingdom of God, and you will be given more. The one who did nothing with his talent was afraid of his master. Many people fail to do anything because they do not see God as a good God.

The question is how do we stay alert, awake and prepared? Jesus declared His purpose for why He lived when as a teenager He said in Luke 2:49: "Did you not know that I must be about My Father's business?" (NKJ) Jesus lives for the purpose of serving His Father. Apostle Paul declared his core value or purpose when he wrote in Phil 3:12 "Not that I have already obtained all this, or have already arrived at my goal, but I press on to take hold of that for which Christ Jesus took hold of me. 13 Brothers and sisters, I do not consider myself yet to have taken hold of it. But one thing I do: Forgetting what is behind and straining toward what is ahead, 14 I press on toward the goal to win the prize for which God has called me heavenward in Christ Jesus." (Phil 3:12-14).

Notice Apostle Paul makes it clear that he expects a prize for having lived a life in obedience to his calling. The goal he is pursuing is laid out in the preceding verse: Phil 3:10 "I want to know Christ—yes, to know the power of his resurrection and participation in his sufferings, becoming like him in his death, 11 and so, somehow, attaining to the resurrection from the dead." The goal is not merely to plant churches, but it is to know Him, and to know Him is also to participate in His suffering. Paul's core value was to spend his life pursuing Jesus that he might experience all that Jesus has for him.

The way Jesus and Paul stayed on course was to have a clear purpose and some set of core values. Here are some of the values I live by:

-I will love Jesus and enjoy His presence.

-I will love what Jesus loves.

-I will love His word and live by it.

-I will love my wife and my family as Jesus loves them. I will leave them a legacy.

-I will extend honour and respect even at the expense of being right.

-I will love His church locally and worldwide and find my place in His body.

-I will use the talents given to me for His Kingdom's sake.

-I will give generously to His church in tithes and offerings.

-I will do what I can to see His Kingdom go forth through evangelism.

-I will love the people who do not love me. Jesus loves His enemies:

"Father forgive them."

-I will be quick to forgive and let no one offend me.

-I will love the broken. Luke 4:18 shows Jesus loved the broken hearted.

Matthew 25 teaches us to love the poor and prisoners.

-I will trust God for my needs. I will not work for a wage; I will work for His Kingdom. According to Matthew 6:33, I will seek His kingdom and His righteousness.

-I will enjoy life and His creation.

-I will walk in His power and not in my own strength. I will eagerly pursue His gifts.

-I will want Jesus to tell me as in 2 Timothy 4: 7 (You) have fought the good fight, you have finished the race, you have kept the faith.

-I will be honest with myself, telling Jesus and a few chosen people what goes on in my heart.

We stay alert by living by some core values as God told Joshua: 7 "Be strong and very courageous. Be careful to obey all the law my servant Moses gave you; do not turn from it to the right or to the left, that you may be successful wherever you go. 8 Keep this Book of the Law always on your lips; meditate on it day and night, so that you may prosperous. (Joshua 1-7-8)

When I was kid, maybe 6 years of age, my mother had baked some fresh cookies and locked them in jar in a cabinet. I knew where the key was and found my fingers in the jar sneaking a few cookies. This naturally did not stop with a few so when my mother came to retrieve some for the visitors, the jar was half empty or less, and she asked me if I had done it. I said, "No". My dad was called, and he asked the same question, and I repeated my answer, "No". I got a spanking and was sent to bed. The message was clear: "I am not giving you this spanking because you took the cookies, but because you lied," my dad said, looking me straight in the eyes. I still remember this rebuke to this day. My dad imparted core values into me and since then, when confronted with whether I did something or not, I always tell the truth because I remember the consequence of not doing it. The same way God imparts core values into us so that our decisions will lead to preparedness for the coming King.

Core values help us make decisions. One of those decisions is how to use our skills, money and influence for the Kingdom. When Jesus is telling the disciples to be His witnesses, He is telling us to do the same. This means that one of our core values shall be to pour our talents into local and foreign missions.

What core values might your parents have instilled in you?

What core values did Jesus impart in the disciples?

What talents might you have that God wants you to use to further His kingdom?

24. Alert the Church!

Read the Gospel of Mark Chapter 14

Mark 13:5" Jesus said to them: "Watch out that no one deceives you. 6 Many will come in my name, claiming, 'I am he,' and will deceive many. 7 When you hear of wars and rumours of wars, do not be alarmed. Such things must happen, but the end is still to come." 24 and all are justified freely by his grace through the redemption that came by Christ Jesus. Jesus reminds us through chapter 13 to be alert, to watch and to be on guard so that we may not miss His second coming. Jesus reminds us in Mark 14 through the Lord's Supper that He will not drink the wine again until He comes back. Jesus moulds us so that when He comes, "We will be like Him because we will see Him as He is." 1 John 3:2 The Pharisees missed His first coming because of their hardened hearts, their unbelief and their failure to repent. Let us not fall asleep and miss His second coming.

I have shared about different core values that can keep us as individuals awake and alert, but what about the church, how can it keep from falling asleep? When Jesus talks to the seven churches in Revelation, He rebukes six of them. The Ephesian church lost its first love, the Church of Laodicea became lukewarm. The others tolerated sin. What about us, what will Jesus tell our church?

What about you? What would Jesus say to you, are you ready to meet Jesus? In Ephesians5:2, Jesus tells us that He is coming for a radiant church, a church without spot or wrinkle, a church washed by the word. In Mark 13, Jesus tells us that we are to be on guard against deception, that we need to stand firm during persecution, be strong, and not be overwhelmed by catastrophes both natural and manmade. The purpose of the church, He tells us, is to evangelize the world. One of the ways for the church to be strong is to become a body. In North America we have become very individualistic. It is all about, me, myself and God, no one else. No need for church. One Sunday, I mentioned that we are independent, and I heard myself say, "It is all about me, myself and my dog, no one else." I wondered now why I said dog when I had intended to say God. After the service, a lady came up to me and told me that this very morning on the way to church, she had said those very words to herself, "Me, myself and my dog, I don't need church." God spoke to her through those words. She had just about believed a lie, but instead she walked out that day with, "Yes, I do need this church." We can watch church online, but it is not the same as being part of a body of believers.

Jesus is the Head and we are His body. A hand cut off the arm soon turns blue and becomes ineffective. However, a hand connected to an arm, that in turn is connected to a body and a body that is connected to a head becomes very effective. In 1 Cor. 12, Paul reminds us that no part of the body is less valuable than other parts. A janitor is as valuable as the preacher is. Together as one, we grow to become like Him. What joins the limbs together is not the law, but love. Eph 4: 15 "Instead, speaking the truth in love, we will grow to become in every respect the mature body of him who is the head, that is, Christ.16 From him the whole body, joined and held together by every supporting ligament, grows and builds itself up in love, as each part does its work." Plug into a church. Become part of it.

One day I read Forgotten God by Francis Chan, and he compared the church of today with the story of Elijah confronting Ahab and Jezebel's Baal prophets on Mount Carmel. (Page 143) Ahab and Jezebel had killed off many of the prophets of God and replaced them with Baal prophets. Elijah felt he was one of the few believers in the God of Abraham, Isaac and Jacob left. When he comes out of hiding, he challenges Ahab to bring his 450 Baal prophets and all of Israel to the mountain. Baal worshippers built an altar and placed a bull on it, and then spent all morning dancing and crying out for fire to fall. No fire fell. The church of today is like that, dancing and making so much noise. We need to come with expectations of people being changed, healed, delivered, or transformed. When Elijah's turn came and he earnestly prayed, the fire fell and consumed the meat. The response was: 39 "When all the people saw this, they fell prostrate and cried, "The Lord—he is God! The Lord—he is God!"(1 Kings 18:39) May people at the end of our church service leave saying, "The Lord-He is God."

We want people at the end of our church services to respond with: "This is the Lord!" If it is a good church service, rather than the response being, 'what good worship' or 'that was a wonderful sermon,' we want to hear "This is God!!" An alert church is one that is a good steward of His presence. The point is not to get through a program but to follow the leading of the Holy Spirit. The church makes room for what the Holy Spirit wants to do. The sermons are words of revelation flowing from heaven. The worship leaders are sensitive to what songs to sing and what God wants to do in the service. It is a church that is willing to take risks and use the gifts like Words of Knowledge and healing. Just as Elijah prayed and the fire came so does the presence of God come when we as a body stand in agreement with what Jesus wants to do.

This is what the Bible says about Elijah in James 5: 17" Elijah was a human being, even as we are. He prayed earnestly that it would not rain, and it did not rain on the land for three and a half years. 18 Again he prayed, and the heavens gave rain, and the earth produced its crops." A church alive with His presence is a church that prays earnestly. The house of the Lord is a house of prayer. To be awake we need to spend time in prayer together and individually. We need to listen and to declare His promises over our church and one another.

I just re-read the book called The Heavenly Man by Paul Hattaway. Brother Yun spent many years imprisoned in China for having preached the gospel. Brother Yun, whose life the book is all about, just spoke recently in a community close by. Brother Yun was born in China in 1958. The churches had been burned and missionaries had been sent home under Mao`s cultural revolution. His mother had heard the gospel in 1940 but had forgotten her faith until her husband got severely ill. Jesus revealed himself to her in a dream and told her that He loved her. The next day she put her hand on her husband and prayed to the One in her dream. Miraculously her husband was healed. The whole family became believers. However, they had no bibles, nor did they have a church. Yun wanted a bible desperately. He went and asked a man who had served as a pastor before the revolution. This man was afraid and told Yun that he had to ask God for one. For a hundred days, Yun prayed, eating only a bowl of rice every day. On the hundredth day, he had a dream that someone would come with some bread and when he took a bite, the loaf turned into a bible. The next day two men stood at the door and said, 'we have some bread for you!' In their bag was a bible.

Although Yun only had a grade three education, he memorized all 28 chapters of Matthew. He then felt that God told him to go to the East and the South to preach. The next day he went to the East and when he came upon a village, he discovered that they had already been waiting for him. He did not know how to preach so he closed his eyes and recited all the Scriptures he had remembered. He did not know if they could follow or could understand. But when he opened his eyes, he saw the village repenting and turning their hearts over to Jesus. Yun discovered the power of the living Word. This became the first among thousands of churches he started. Yun became a leader of the underground church that today has spread all over China. About 35,000 are saved every day. I read that they figure by 2025 there will be more Christians in China than in any other country in the world. Of course, the government did not like this. The enemy came against Yun and everyone who believed, imprisoning them, torturing them and starving their families. The greatest temptation came when the government decided to be friendly to the West and so offered the Christians to join government-sanctioned churches. Yun, together with many other leaders, said, 'No', knowing that the government-sanctioned church would compromise the gospel. In other words, the message of Jesus being the Messiah and the Son of the living God would be compromised. Because they refused to compromise the Word, the church is growing like wildfire in a country where the government is opposing it. Nevertheless, the gates of hell will not prevail.

Yun became imprisoned many times and escaped frequently. Finally, they put him in maximum security in Peking and to prevent him from escaping they broke both his legs. One night God told him that the next day he would walk out of the prison. The next morning, he called upon the guard to go the washroom which entailed another prisoner to carry him. By the time they got into the hallway he found that he could walk. He walked past the guards whom God must have blinded. He ended up at a friend's place who was expecting him and found a way to hide him, and eventually he escaped to Germany. When he arrived in Germany as a refugee, he discovered, for the first time, the Western church. This was like nothing that he had ever experienced in China. In China, they would meet after midnight and worship, pray and listen to the Word being taught until morning. In the Western church their services only lasted an hour, with no altar calls, no miracles, no salvation and no expectations of God's power to be released. In China when they took an offering, they emptied their pockets so that a brother could be sent to a nearby village where he was to start a church. In the West, there was no such urgency to reach out. Jesus is coming for a glorious church that prays, believes, expects, and behaves like a body; a Church that is washed by the Word and is a bride without wrinkle or spot.

Help us, Lord, to be that beautiful bride set apart for You.

Let us be alert -- He is coming! Let us be ready!!

Conclusion

It is your call.

This is Martin Luther King Junior's last speech:

"Like anybody, I would like to live a long life. Longevity has its place. But I'm not concerned about that now. I just want to do God's will. And He's allowed me to go up to the mountain. And I have looked over, and I've seen the Promised Land. I may not go there with you, but I want you to know tonight that we as a people will get to the Promised Land. So, I'm happy tonight. I'm not worried about anything. I do not fear any man. 'Mine eyes have seen the glory of the coming of the Lord.'" (From King's last speech, in Memphis, the night before His assassination.) Copied from Soul Survivor by Philip Yancy, (pg. 40.)

I wrote this book so that you would know in your heart who Jesus is and that no matter what you have done, or should have done, you can see by the Spirit the hand of God reaching out for you, telling you that it is your choice, your call, if by faith you grab hold of His hand, and you let go of the things of this world that have enslaved you. You will hear His voice saying, "Follow Me," and when you begin to follow Him you will encounter His love -- the very thing you have been striving for all your life. To follow Him means surrendering your will, your mind, your time, and your possessions. If you read through the Book of Mark chapter by chapter and stop and ask the Lord what He wants you to do, and do it, you will mature.

One day when I was in Kenya, I stood in a pitch-dark mud hut where a single mother stood with her twelve-year-old son who had just purchased ten cents worth of kerosene so we could have a light. I asked the boy what I could pray for, and he answered that I could pray that he could get back into school. I asked him what he needed, and he answered that he needed $75 Canadian to pay his tuition. I reached into my pocket and gave him what I had...it was equal to $75 Canadian! I felt such a love for him and I knew it was God's love.

Because of God's love for you He is reaching out and inviting you to follow Him, but it is your call.

You might say the call you have to make is not about life and death, but it is.

When I said yes to Jesus, He not only gave me eternal life, He also filled me with His love -- the same love that filled Martin Luther King and motivated him to fight for justice.

It is your call! The invitation is an invitation to start a journey following Jesus, bringing the kingdom of God to a fearful and lost generation. God's love transforms people and societies. For that reason, I wrote this book. So, bend your knees, ask Jesus to forgive you for your sins, and ask Him to be the Lord of your life and to fill you with His love. Just watch and see how you begin to long for more of Him and how the Bible becomes alive. Take the next step and begin to share that experience with someone. When you say yes to Jesus, your life becomes interwoven with His.

There is nothing more exciting than that. Bless you with saying yes to His love. You just have to receive by faith.

It is your call.

Apostle Paul's response to his encounter on the Damascus Road in Acts 9 is to ask, "Who are you, Lord, and what must I do?"

5 "Who are you, Lord?" Saul asked. "I am Jesus, whom you are persecuting," he replied. 6 "Now get up and go into the city, and you will be told what you must do."

This book is written to answer those two questions: "Who are you, Lord, and what must I do?" If you pursue answers to those two questions you will partner with God to bring His kingdom to this earth.

There is no more exciting mission in this life!

Manufactured by Amazon.ca
Bolton, ON

28614155R00103